DATE DUE

GAYLORD			PRINTED IN U.S.A.

MODERN WORLD CULTURES

Africa South of the Sahara

◆

Australia and the Pacific

◆

East Asia

◆

Europe

◆

Latin America

◆

North Africa and the Middle East

◆

Northern America

◆

Russia and
the Former Soviet Republics

◆

South Asia

◆

Southeast Asia

◆

This is what the Earth looks like at night. This image is actually a composite of hundreds of pictures made by orbiting satellites. Man-made lights highlight the developed or populated areas of the Earth's surface. The dark areas include the central part of South America, Africa, Asia, and Australia.

(Credit: C. Mayhew and R. Simmon; NASA/GSFC, NOAA/NGDC, DMSP Digital Archive.)

Europe

Zoran Pavlović
Oklahoma State University

Series Consulting Editor
Charles F. Gritzner
South Dakota State University

CHELSEA HOUSE
PUBLISHERS
An imprint of Infobase Publishing

61169822

6/08

Cover: Place du General de Gaulle, Lille, France

Europe

Copyright © 2006 by Infobase Publishing

Chelsea House
An imprint of Infobase Publishing
132 West 31st Street
New York NY 10001

Library of Congress Cataloging-in-Publication Data

Pavlovic, Zoran.
  Europe / Zoran Pavlovic.
    p. cm. — (Modern world cultures)
  Includes bibliographical references and index.
  ISBN 0-7910-8143-5 (hard cover)
  1. Europe—Geography. I. Title. II. Series.
  D900.P38 2005
  940—dc22   2005021756

Text and cover design by Takeshi Takahashi

Printed in the United States of America

Bang MCC 10 9 8 7 6 5 4 3 2 1

This book is printed on acid-free paper.

TABLE OF CONTENTS

Geography is the key that unlocks the door to the world's wonders. There are, of course, many ways of viewing the world and its diverse physical and human features. In this series—MODERN WORLD CULTURES—the emphasis is on people and their cultures. As you step through the geographic door into the ten world cultures covered in this series, you will come to better know, understand, and appreciate the world's mosaic of peoples and how they live. You will see how different peoples adapt to, use, and change their natural environments. And you will be amazed at the vast differences in thinking, doing, and living practiced around the world. The MODERN WORLD CULTURES series was developed in response to many requests from librarians and teachers throughout the United States and Canada.

As you begin your reading tour of the world's major cultures, it is important that you understand three terms that are used throughout the series: geography, culture, and region. These words and their meanings are often misunderstood. **Geography** is an age-old way of viewing the varied features of Earth's surface. In fact, it is the oldest of the existing sciences! People have *always* had a need to know about and understand their surroundings. In times past, a people's world was their immediate surroundings; today, our world is global in scope. Events occuring half a world away can and often do have an immediate impact on our lives. If we, either individually or as a nation of peoples, are to be successful in the global community, it is essential that we know and understand our neighbors, regardless of who they are or where they may live.

Geography and history are similar in many ways; both are methodologies—distinct ways of viewing things and events. Historians are concerned with time, or when events happened. Geographers, on the other hand, are concerned with space, or where things are located. In essence, geographers ask: "What is where, why there, and why care?" in regard to various physical and human features of Earth's surface.

Culture has many definitions. For this series and for most geographers and anthropologists, it refers to a people's *way of life*. This means the totality of everything we possess because we are human, such as our ideas, beliefs, and customs, including language, religious beliefs, and all knowledge. Tools and skills also are an important aspect of culture. Different cultures, after all, have different types of technology and levels of technological attainment that they can use in performing various tasks. Finally, culture includes social interactions—the ways different people interact with one another individually and as groups.

Finally, the idea of **region** is one geographers use to organize and analyze geographic information spatially. A region is an area that is set apart from others on the basis of one or more unifying elements. Language, religion, and major types of economic activity are traits that often are used by geographers to separate one region from another. Most geographers, for example, see a cultural division between Northern, or Anglo, America and Latin America. That "line" is usually drawn at the U.S.-Mexico boundary, although there is a broad area of transition and no actual cultural line exists.

The ten culture regions presented in this series have been selected on the basis of their individuality, or uniqueness. As you tour the world's culture realms, you will learn something of their natural environment, history, and way of living. You will also learn about their population and settlement, how they govern themselves, and how they make their living. Finally, you will take a peek into the future in the hope of identifying each region's challenges and prospects. Enjoy your trip!

Charles F. "Fritz" Gritzner
Department of Geography
South Dakota State University
May 2005

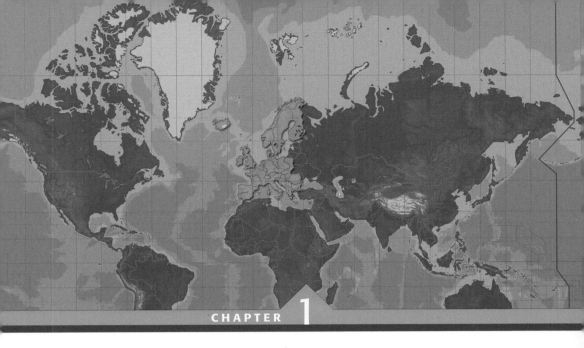

CHAPTER 1

Introducing Europe

The continent of Europe owes its existence and name to the Ancient Greeks. The Greeks were the first to develop the concept of continents. Living on both shores of the Aegean Sea, they created the cultural distinction between Europe (present-day Greece) and Asia (Ionian Greece, or what is now Asiatic Turkey). Peoples of the Eastern Mediterranean followed the seafaring Phoenicians in recognizing *Asu* (sunrise) and *Ereb* (sunset). For the Greeks, this logically translated into the lands that lay on the eastern shore of the Aegean Sea, where the sun rose, being called Asia and those on the west, on the Greek Peninsula, where the sun set, being called Europe.

The town of Kapsali, located off the coast of Greece, sits on the Island of Kythira. Europe is often called a "peninsula of peninsulas," with much of its land protruding into the Atlantic Ocean and Mediterranean Sea.

Colonial expansion throughout the Mediterranean and Black Sea basins during the first millennium B.C. resulted in the widespread idea of distinct continents. Greek mythology is important in understanding the link between Ereb and Europe. In the mythological context, Europa was a woman who, after being taken by Zeus to the island of Crete, was worshiped as a goddess. They had three children. Europa then married the local ruler on Crete, who adopted her sons and integrated divine blood into the Minoan dynasty.

This book is less concerned with the mythological aspects of the European culture region than with the practical. The focus is on the wide array of cultural elements that make this part of the world so unique. It also explains why geographers and others find Europe fascinating and attempts to paint a clear picture of the similarities and differences between Europeans and people of other world cultures. What is it that sets Europeans apart from Africans, Asians, and others? To answer such questions, we must look at the land, the people, and the people's way of life. We must attempt to understand how European culture evolved over many millennia on this small, relatively isolated peninsula. To understand the present, we must always look to the past, for there lie the roots of contemporary patterns of living.

A PENINSULA OF PENINSULAS

Compared with continental giants such as Asia and Africa, Europe is rather small: Its area is comparable to that of the United States. Europe hardly qualifies as a continent in terms of its physical geography. There is no clear physical "division" that separates Europe from Asia. Rather, Europe is a relatively small peninsular appendage of the huge Eurasian landmass. Culturally, however, Europe is quite different from other lands. On this basis alone, it stands apart as both a continent and as a distinct culture realm. As you will learn in this book, Europe's physical features have played an interesting role in terms of cultural development and adaptation.

Europe is often called a "peninsula of peninsulas." In the north, Scandinavia and Jutland are appendages to the main peninsula. Iberia juts southwestward between the Atlantic Ocean and the Mediterranean Sea. Within the Mediterranean, Italy and Greece occupy peninsulas of great historical importance. As a result of Europe's many protrusions, no point on the continent is more than 300 miles (500 kilometers) from salt water. Through time, this factor alone has been of tremendous physical, cultural, and historical importance to the region.

The general east-west alignment of Europe's higher mountain ranges also has been an extremely important geographical factor. There are no mountain barriers to block the prevailing westerly winds that sweep across the continent from the Atlantic Ocean. As a result, almost the entire continent receives ample moisture and has a moderate marine climate. Such conditions provide comfortable and enjoyable living free of aridity, extreme droughts, or severe temperatures. Much of Europe has climatic conditions similar to those in coastal California and Oregon. This type of environment is extremely attractive to most people. In addition to the pleasant climate, much of Europe's terrain is plains or hills that lie at relatively low elevation. These lands are easy to farm, build on, and traverse. This is one of several factors that have helped Europe become the most densely populated continent.

CRADLE OF MODERN CIVILIZATION

The Middle East, particularly Mesopotamia, in present-day Iraq, is regarded as the "cradle of Western Civilization." Within this area, early civilizations began to flourish several millennia B.C. These early high cultures were based primarily on plant and animal domestication, the rise of cities, and the development of strong institutions. From here, traits such as written language, mathematics, and astronomy began to spread elsewhere, including westward into Europe.

In terms of more recent cultural impact, Europe has been the center of cultural growth and change. Today, we speak of the "European culture" that dominates throughout the New World—North America, South America, and Australia. During the first millennium B.C., the Ancient Greeks colonized the Mediterranean world, diffusing (spreading) their culture to others. Later, in much of Europe, the Middle East, and North Africa, Roman cultural influence spread. During the past five centuries, European colonial powers have transformed the local cultures in all corners of our world.

To understand the magnitude of this impact, we need but look at the United States. Here, the majority of the population is of European descent, and nearly all Americans today, regardless of ancestral origin, practice a way of life with European roots. This is one reason we feel so "at home" when traveling in Europe. Our language, religion, dining habits, and social interactions are European in origin, as is democracy, which is cherished by the United States. Our market-oriented, free-enterprise economy is also European in origin. In an attempt to create a highly civilized society, the Founding Fathers tried to recreate the best from European culture.

THE BORDERS OF THE EUROPEAN CULTURE REGION

Today, considerable confusion exists over where and what, precisely, is "Europe." It is not at all uncommon to find statistical data organized by continents, with Europe, Asia, *and* Russia represented. If Russia is included as a part of Europe, data often pertain to all of the country, including the vast area of Siberia that lies entirely in Asia. When using European data, one must first determine the geographic area to which they pertain.

Europe is surrounded on three sides by huge bodies of water: the Arctic Ocean to the north, the Atlantic Ocean to the west, and the Mediterranean and the Black seas to the south. These physical features clearly form a border between Europe and other continental landmasses in three directions. The Strait of Gibraltar, a rather narrow passage, is a definite physical and cultural border between the European and North African culture realms. A short ferry ride across the strait from Spain to Morocco places one in a vastly different culture world. Although these realms are not divided by great distance, a sharp cultural boundary is easily identified and defined. Differences in language, religion, food, and customs are obvious to even the casual observer. North Africans are not of Indo-European stock as most Europeans are. Ethnically, most Moroccans are much more closely related to Middle Easterners than they are to Spaniards or other Europeans.

The eastern border of Europe is much more difficult to define because there is no sharp physical or cultural boundary to mark the line. Most geographers have arbitrarily chosen to use the Ural mountain range as the point that separates Europe and Asia. In other contexts, the boundary between the two continents depends more on cultural and political conditions than on physical geography.

Placing Russia in the scheme of continental divisions poses a great dilemma. Most Westerners tend to think of Russia as being in the "Orient" rather than as part of Europe. The country has a long history of contact with and influence from groups such as Mongol invaders and others from the "Stans" of central Asia. There also have been close ties with the Eastern Roman (Byzantine) Empire and Orthodox Christianity. To Western Europeans, Russians seem to be a world apart and much less "European" than themselves.

Throughout much of history, the Don River (in present-day Ukraine) was used as the continental borderline. As Russian (and later, Soviet) strength grew, the border kept moving eastward. After the dissolution of the Soviet Union in the early 1990s, however, many newly independent countries began to look westward. Based particularly on cultural links, they claim a European heritage. Cultural traits—religion is one of the most important—play a vital role in defining continental borders. Countries such as Georgia and Armenia maintain that, because they are among the world's oldest Christian countries, they should be accepted as European. Turkey, in contrast, is often considered a non-European country because more than 90 percent of its territory is on the eastern side of the water link between the Black and Mediterranean seas. A small portion of the country, including its capital city, Istanbul, is in Europe.

Regions do not exist in reality. Geographers (and others) "invent" them based on certain characteristics and needs. It is best to think of regions as "convenience packages" that are used to organize and analyze geographical information. By definition, a region must possess one or more homogeneous elements. The regional concept helps us make sense of the world by dividing various cultural and natural features into similar and dissimilar areas.

This book is another product of geographers' attempts to organize the world into regions for the benefit of you, the reader. Arbitrarily, the eastern boundary is drawn between Poland and Ukraine. This separates all of the former Soviet Union from the rest of Central and Western Europe. Why was this done? Estonia, Latvia, and Lithuania have long-standing ties with Europe, so why aren't they included in this book? This is the kind of decision geographers must make. It was decided that all countries that were once a part of the Soviet Union would be covered in a different volume in this series. Simply stated, Kazakhstan has more in common with Ukraine than it does with France or Ireland.

Geographers think spatially, asking, in essence, "What is where, why there, and why care?" in regard to the various physical and human features of Earth's surface. Culture itself is an anthropological concept. You might rightfully ask, then, why geographers are working with the idea. Culture—whether individual traits such as religion or language, or trait groupings such as the European way of life—is distributed spatially. That is to say, all aspects of culture are found some*where;* therefore, the study of culture is also geographical. Geographers do not only organize information spatially; like historians, they also look to the past to understand the present and project into the future.

As mentioned previously, regions are convenience packages. They organize information to make it more meaningful as people attempt to better understand the world. In this book, you will learn about the European ways of life. The region as a whole shares much in common, but within Europe there is great diversity. Scandinavians are not like Sicilians, Poles are not like Portuguese, and the British have a lifestyle different from that of Bulgarians. Hierarchical patterns often exist within cultures; therefore, Europe can be divided into a number of subregions on a cultural basis. Southern Europe is set apart from other regions of the continent. There is a distinct Mediterranean culture realm, but it, too, can be further divided into a number of subregions, including the Iberian Peninsula. Even here, some differences exist between Spaniards and Portuguese, and within Spain, there are the Basques, who do not consider themselves Spaniards.

EUROPE'S GLOBAL ROLE

For centuries, the United Kingdom, France, Spain, and the Netherlands were the most powerful countries in the world. Their reach extended far beyond national boundaries. Spanish kings controlled a vast empire in the Americas, and the United Kingdom possessed an empire on which the sun never set. Napoleon Bonaparte of France conquered almost the entire European continent. At the time when the United States was in its infancy, Europe was the center of world power whether political, military, or cultural. The Industrial Revolution in the nineteenth century solidly established (Western) Europe as the world leader in economic development, education, democratic institutions, and technology. Because of Europe's worldwide network of colonial possessions, European culture spanned the globe. Europe's leadership waned as colonies were lost, its lands and peoples were ravaged by wars, and the United States grew into the world's leading superpower. The twentieth century clearly belonged to Americans.

Europe is regaining much of its lost prominence. The European Union (EU) is rapidly expanding, and the regional economy is gaining strength. No longer is strength based on competition and colonial exploitation; rather, it is the result of regional cooperation and integration. European countries are no longer perceived as imperialists and colonialists as they were during the nineteenth and early twentieth centuries. Their global role has changed greatly. Today, they share their wealth

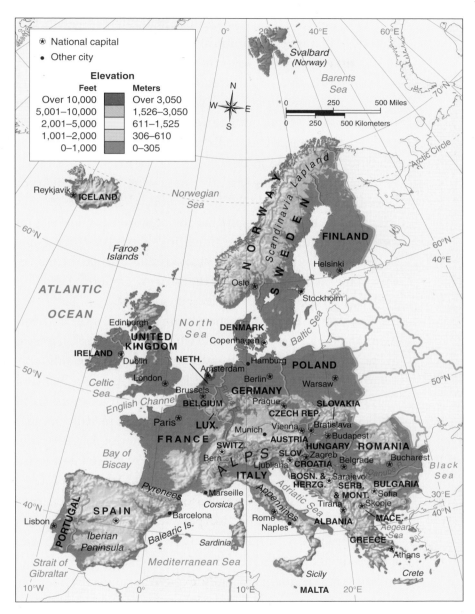

This is a general political map of Europe. Note that most areas of Europe are located at, or slightly above, sea level.

and try to improve the lives of people, including those in former colonies. The global community now looks to Europe as a moral leader—one that leads by example.

The unification of Europe, which was unimaginable until recently, is about to become a reality. Former Communist countries such as Poland, Hungary, and Slovenia are now entering the European Union. Other nations are standing in line ready to join as soon as possible. If successful, European integration will eventually lead to integration at a global level. Countries will be ready for the previously unthinkable: They will give up their sovereignty for the common good of the region. Perhaps the world is on the brink of an innovative global political organization that is originating in Europe. Details of this remarkable political development, including how it evolved into the present structure, are discussed in Chapter 6.

Geography is often described as a "bridge" that links humans and their ways of life to the natural environment. Cultural geographers study the various ways in which humans culturally adapt to, use, and change the physical places in which they live. Ways of life vary throughout Europe based on location. Some of these differences can be explained, at least in part, because Europe, like any other cultural region, is not uniform. People in remote mountain areas of Southeastern Europe have developed different cultural characteristics than those who live in large industrial cities of the North European Plain. Chapter 2 provides detailed information about the ways in which Europeans have interacted with their varied environments. The natural environment does not "determine" culture; rather, it is through culture that humans make the environment useful. The Netherlands serves as a wonderful example. People there had limited space and very few natural resources. Today, much of the country's area—including extremely productive agricultural land—was "stolen" from the sea. People now live, livestock now graze, and crops now grow on land that formerly was the floor of the North Sea!

Chapter 3 provides an overview of Europe's very complex culture history and is followed by a chapter on population and settlement. In Chapter 5, you will learn about contemporary European culture and society, including topics such as language, religion, social relations, and ethnicity. Chapters 6 and 7 are devoted to the region's extremely complex political history and economy, respectively. In Chapter 8, you will visit Europe's subregions, including a stop in the most important countries, cities, and other features. It provides a regional summary of the various topics covered elsewhere in the book. Finally, the journey concludes with a glimpse into the future of the European culture region.

CHAPTER 2

Physical Geography

Geographers use the term *landscape* to describe the appearance of an area—a landscape represents what we see. In terms of Earth's physical features, we talk about physical landscapes or all things on Earth that are not of human origin. Examples include landform features such as glaciated mountains, rolling hills, and monotonous plains. Water features are a part of the natural landscape, as are forests and grasslands. Once the human imprint on the land becomes visible, the features that result from it become part of the cultural landscape as well.

It can be argued that pristine (pure) natural landscapes no longer exist because humans have left their imprint in even the most remote areas of Earth. Certainly, this is true for most, if not all, of Europe.

Humans have been hunting, burning, digging, and cutting for hundreds of thousands of years. Human societies use the environment to fit their needs (not the other way around) by choosing where and how to live. The force that changes the way we live is cultural, not environmental, in origin. Our culture provides us with the tools, techniques, and skills to interact with the natural environment.

Even today, however, many books describe how the natural environment strongly influences, or even determines, the ways people live. Have you ever heard reference to "desert peoples," or "rain-forest peoples"? These terms suggest that all people in those environments live in pretty much the same way. The tendency to create a picture of humans (and their culture) as subject to nature is widespread and difficult to change.

Nature cannot "speak" to us, and it cannot tell us what to do. Only humans, with their cultural "bag of tricks" (amassed knowledge), can bestow meaning and value to an environment. Nowhere is this more evident than in terms of economic interests. With the development of effective and inexpensive air conditioning, Phoenix, Arizona—previously judged to be too hot—suddenly became one of the country's fastest-growing cities. The coldest inhabited region in the world, Siberia, develops rapidly wherever oil or natural gas is discovered. Humans sometimes lose a battle against nature (flooding, fires, landslides, and so on), but they always win wars. Cultural determinism is the concept that many geographers use to discuss cultural ecology. It places humans, acting as cultural agents, at the fore in understanding and explaining the relationship between people and the environments that they occupy. Perhaps nowhere else in the world is the idea of cultural determinism better illustrated than in Europe. This chapter presents an overview of Europe's physical geographic conditions and provides examples of cultural adaptation within the region.

Karst topography, resulting from solution weathering of limestone or dolomite rock, dominates the landscape in many Mediterranean locations.

LANDFORM FEATURES

As a result of the movement of tectonic plates (pieces of Earth's crust), especially the African plate crashing into southern Europe, the continent has some interesting geologic characteristics. There are a number of peninsulas and several major mountain ranges, both young and old, as well as rolling hills, basins, and plains that cover large areas of northern Europe.

Mountains

Mountain ranges in North America have a north-south orientation and can be difficult to cross. In Europe, the major ranges trend in an east-west direction and are lower, offering a number of easily traversed passes. These passes served as a cultural

highway between the northern and southern areas for centuries. Today, they are the routes followed by many highways
and railroads. The once-feared German invaders of Rome have
been replaced with another form of German invader: Modern
visitors are not pillagers, but rather tourists who use these
alpine passageways to flood Italy in search of fun, history, and a
different culture.

Although roughly comparable in height to the American
Rocky Mountains and Sierra Nevada, the Alps hardly present a
huge barrier. Mont Blanc, the highest point in Europe (not
including Russia), is located in France. The peak soars to 15,781
feet (4,819 meters), making it slightly higher than any mountain in the continental United States. Low passes through the
Alps have been used for millennia. Where needed, lengthy
tunnels have been dug, even through the highest mountains, to
connect countries. The longest of all, the St. Gotthard Tunnel,
built in 1980, connects Switzerland and Italy. It is 10.2 miles
(16.4 kilometers) long, and it serves as a railroad and automo-
bile tunnel. To the east, in Austria and Slovenia, the Alps are
lower. Broad glacial and river valleys form additional traffic
corridors and space for many settlements, including substantial
cities such as Innsbruck and Vienna.

As is the case with other European mountainous areas, the
Alps have been inhabited since prehistoric times. Each group of
people has left its mark. This is particularly noticeable in various religious festivals that take place in Alpine countries. Many
Christian events in Austria, Germany, and Switzerland incor-
porate a mixture of Germanic and Slavic pagan elements. These
ancient traits of folk culture survived for thousands of years in
remote highland valleys and villages. Throughout Europe,
people who live in mountainous areas have preserved many
unique cultural characteristics or traditional folkways.

In the Pyrenees—the range that forms a natural boundary
between France and the Iberian Peninsula—Basques have
thrived in relative isolation for thousands of years. Located high

The Alps spread from France to Austria and for centuries have served as both a physical and cultural boundary between northern Europe and the Mediterranean.

in the Pyrenees, the tiny country of Andorra is a popular tourist destination. Throughout most of its history, however, this microstate was able to survive because of its isolated mountain location. The Pyrenees are much more difficult to pass through than the Alps. Neither rivers nor glaciers opened wide valleys or low passes, so the area is easily defended from invaders. Many peoples used these mountains as a refuge. One of the best-known examples is a religious sect known as the Cathars. These people took refuge in the Pyrenees during the thirteenth century to escape papal persecution. Christian Crusaders were sent by the pope to root out the Cathars and destroy them. The Cathars were able to retreat deep into the mountains, where, using caves and fortifications, they were able to defend themselves from persecution or even death. Until recent decades, when modern technology provided roads and tunnels, the Pyrenees were perhaps the most isolated area in Western Europe.

In Southeastern Europe, several nations owe their survival to the fact that the people retreated to the mountains. Albanians, for example, are descendants of ancient Illyrians, who once controlled large areas between the Adriatic Sea and present-day Bulgaria. Ultimately, they were pushed by stronger Slavs (and later Turks) into the most isolated parts of the Dinaric Alps. A majority of them still lives there today. Northern Albania may be the most culturally isolated area in all of Europe. Lacking strong outside influences, remote villagers still consider a tribal set of norms, established in the fifteenth century by a local feudal ruler, the only form of law. This set of norms has its roots in ancient codes of honor that include cultural traits such as blood feuds and arranged marriages. When living in a natural environment that provides cultural isolation from the outside world, people tend to develop unique culture elements. Many such traits are preserved for a long period of time and are difficult to change.

Other major mountain ranges in Europe include the Carpathians (from Slovakia to Romania), Apennines (in Italy), Kjölen (in Norway and Sweden), Rhodopes and Pindus (in Bulgaria and Greece), and various ranges in Spain. Between mountains and plains, the European continent is covered with rolling hills. Their elevation is too low for them to be considered mountains but not low and flat enough for them to be considered lowlands. In terms of geologic age, most of the hilly areas are much older and more worn down than the younger mountain ranges, similar to the Appalachian Mountains in the United States. The best known are the Massif Central and Bretagne in France, the Hercynian hills in Germany and Czech Republic, and several areas of Great Britain. In Wales, the Cambrian Mountains are the geologic standard for "ancient." *Precambrian* simply means "earlier than recorded geologic history," or more than about half a billion years old.

Plains

Lowland plains cover the largest area of the European culture region and are home to the greatest number of Europeans. The North European Plain begins at the northern foot of the Pyrenees and extends in an arc through western France and the Low Countries (Belgium and the Netherlands) and into northern Germany and Poland. From there, it opens like an eastward-facing cornucopia, becoming the East European Plain, extending all the way to the Ural Mountains. This wide corridor is populated by several hundred million people, many of whom live in large urban areas such as Hamburg, Bremen, Hanover, Berlin, and Warsaw. Separated from the North European Plain by the Carpathian Mountains is the Pannonian, or Hungarian, Plain. This extremely flat plain was once the floor of the Pannonian Sea. It occupies much of Hungary and extends into several neighboring countries. The Walachian Plain in Romania and the lowlands in northern Italy are the broad valleys of two major rivers: the Danube and the Po. As in the rest of Europe, a majority of these countries' populations resides in the lowland.

Madrid, Paris, and London are all located on plains. The Paris basin is perhaps the most famous because it represents the heart of the French nation and of Western Europe. This relatively small basin is home to more than 10 million people. Just across the English Channel ("La Manche" to the French) and beyond the towering White Cliffs of Dover, lies London, the center of British government, economy, and culture. Paris and London were built in geographically sensitive locations that were well connected to the interior as well as to the Atlantic Ocean via waterways. Finally, although much of Scandinavia is covered by rugged terrain, most people—including those in the capital cities of Oslo, Stockholm, and Helsinki—live on plains.

WEATHER AND CLIMATE

In terms of weather (short-term atmospheric condition) and climate (long-term average weather conditions), Europe has

Miles of sand beaches and dunes along France's Atlantic coast represent a type of landscape not seen elsewhere in Europe.

several prominent characteristics. First, it is located in the temperate middle latitudes, with most of the continent between 40 and 60 degrees north latitude. Second, because of its peninsular shape, most of the continent benefits from the temperature-moderating influence of the sea and receives adequate moisture. Third, much of the continent lies at a relatively low elevation, which keeps temperatures warmer. Finally, the east-west orientation of major mountain ranges allows for the penetration of moisture-bearing winds and also large air masses off the Atlantic Ocean and from Siberia in Eastern Europe. Overall, most of Europe enjoys a climate that is relatively mild and adequately moist. Nowhere in this region do world-record weather conditions occur.

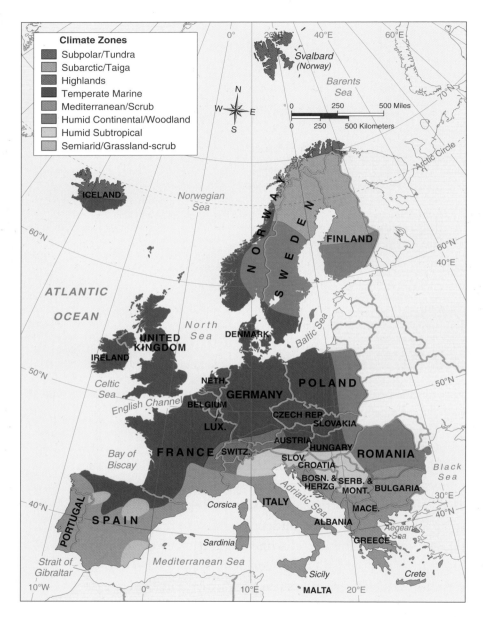

Climate Zones
- Subpolar/Tundra
- Subarctic/Taiga
- Highlands
- Temperate Marine
- Mediterranean/Scrub
- Humid Continental/Woodland
- Humid Subtropical
- Semiarid/Grassland-scrub

This map shows the distribution of different climates throughout Europe. Surrounded mostly by water, Europe's most prevalent climate zones are Temperate Marine and Mediterrranean/Scrub.

Western Europe

Western Europe is often exposed to the low-pressure air masses that move in from the Atlantic. This mild, soggy air can cover portions of the continent with an overcast sky and drizzling rain for weeks on end, particularly during the fall and winter months. Conditions are similar to those of coastal Oregon, Washington, and British Columbia in North America. Temperatures rarely fall below freezing, and near the coasts, snow is infrequent. Prevailing westerly winds block the penetration of cold air masses from Asia. Precipitation can last for weeks at a time, but rain is generally light and the total amount of precipitation may be less in Western Europe than in other areas of the region. Temperature ranges do not vary greatly between winter and summer months. Perhaps the best example of this climate is a typical British landscape as it appears in motion pictures: a dreary sky, persistent drizzle, and lush green vegetation. Cloudless days are rare, even during the summer months. In Western Europe, fewer sunny days occur than elsewhere on the continent. During the summer months, violent storms with drenching rain and howling winds occasionally strike the British Isles and France.

Eastern Europe

Moving into the continent's interior, away from the Atlantic Ocean's moderating influence, climate conditions slowly change. Oceanic influences diminish, and air masses that originate over Eurasia have a greater effect. Summer temperatures are considerably higher, and winter temperatures drop much lower than in Western Europe. Conditions are generally somewhat drier than along the coast, and during winter months, precipitation frequently falls as snow. During winter months, a high-pressure system centered over central Siberia generates a strong flow of cold air toward Europe. When this system is well developed, conditions can become quite unpleasant, with temperatures dropping well below freezing for several weeks. Lakes, rivers, and even the Baltic Sea can be frozen for several months during the long winter season. Eastern Europe experiences weather conditions similar to those found in North America, from the Dakotas eastward to New England, although Eastern Europe lacks the extremes that occur in North America.

Southern Europe

Southern Europe, from Portugal to Greece and Turkey, enjoys a mild Mediterranean climate. Its American equivalent is the climate of coastal Southern California from San Diego to San Francisco. Many people consider the Mediterranean the world's most ideal climate. It lacks extremes and is pleasant throughout the year. The Mediterranean region is unique in that it has the only climate that experiences a summer that is drier than the winter. In fact, weeks can pass in the Mediterranean climate without a cloud in the sky and months can pass without a drop of precipitation. Summers are warm, sunny, and dry. Winters are cool and wet, with most, if not all, precipitation falling as rain rather than snow. In mountains, however, snow can be frequent. Once again, the lack of temperature extremes during both summer and winter months reflects the modifying influence of large bodies of water. In the summer months, the sea remains cool and thus cools the atmosphere. July daytime temperatures in the region average a pleasant 77° to 82°F (25° to 27.7°C).

During the winter, the sea is warmer than the adjacent land and it warms the atmosphere. This is particularly obvious in coastal areas of Italy and Croatia, where variations in temperature between the coast and only ten miles inland can be drastic. For most of the Mediterranean climatic region, January temperatures average a comfortable 50°F (10°C). Despite its dry summer conditions, much of the region receives between 40 and 60 inches (100 to 150 centimeters) of precipitation and even more in some places. Lands that border the eastern Adriatic Sea, for example, receive 60 to 80 inches (150 to 200 centimeters). Only a few areas in Spain receive less than 20 inches (50 centimeters) of precipitation.

Northern Europe and Mountain Ranges

Cold climates are limited to northern Scandinavia and high mountain regions such as in the Alps, Pyrenees, and Carpathians. In the north, climatic characteristics are somewhat unique because of the higher latitude. Here, shorter hours of winter sunlight contribute to long, cold, relatively dark winters when compared with those of the rest of the continent. Cold Arctic air masses also work their way southward during the winter, frequently bringing bone-chilling low temperatures to the area. Hundreds of miles to the south, in high mountains, the climate is quite similar to those conditions found in the Arctic fringe, although elevation replaces latitude as the influencing factor.

The alpine, or mountain, climate differs from others because air temperature decreases with increased elevation (this explains the presence of snow and even glaciers atop equatorial peaks in South America and Africa). For every 1,000 feet (305 meters) of increase in altitude, air becomes cooler by 3.5°F (1.5°C). Winters last longer in the Alps, and average temperatures are lower throughout the year.

Other factors are also at work in mountainous areas. As wind blows over a mountain, the air cools, condensation occurs, and precipitation falls on the windward side of the barrier. On the downwind, or rain-shadow, side of the mountain, conditions are much drier. Mountain weather varies in response to these and other local conditions. In Europe and elsewhere in the Northern Hemisphere, most ski resorts are located on the northern or eastern side of mountains. Because of greater exposure to the sun, south-facing slopes have higher temperatures. Snow will not accumulate to as great a depth or last as long as it will on a north-facing slope.

You are now familiar with both the landform and climate conditions of Europe. Mountains, according to environmental determinists, are supposed to be "home of lost causes." They are remote, cold, and difficult to develop. According to theory, people who live in mountainous regions are supposed to be poor and backward. Switzerland, however, located in the heart of the Alps, is one of the world's wealthiest, best-educated, and most successful countries by almost any measure. The same can be said about far-northern, cold, mountainous Norway. In both locations, people have culturally overcome environmental "obstacles" to achieve some of the world's highest living standards. They learned long ago how to use and benefit from the land and resources that surround them. Mountains, which represent a hard reality in Bolivia, for example, are a moneymaking opportunity in Switzerland. Climate and other elements of the natural landscape handicap or help people only to the degree that their culture allows it to happen. Mao Tse-tung once said that "there is no such thing as unproductive lands, there are only unproductive people."

WATER FEATURES

The European culture region possesses an abundant variety of water features. As a result, this region has the world's best-integrated system of inland waterways. This factor is of particular importance in terms of trade and commerce, because transportation of goods by water is by far the least expensive method. Also, except for a few small countries (Switzerland, Slovenia, and Macedonia, for example) nearly every European country has an exit to the world's seas. For some, access is direct through a port city. For others, access to the global sea is gained through an integrated network of navigable rivers and canals.

Rivers

The most important water passage through the continent is formed by the combined Rhine-Main-Danube river route. This system connects the Black Sea with the North Sea by splitting the continent in half, drastically reducing transportation costs. Rotterdam, located in the Netherlands at the mouth of the Rhine River and on the North Sea, is the world's leading seaport. Canals connect the Rhine with the Seine and Rhône rivers in France, thereby creating links to the Mediterranean Sea and the English Channel.

Lakes and Fjords

As a result of ice-age continental glaciations, Europe is covered by a large number of lakes, especially in the northern rim, where the results of glaciation are the most visible. The landscape of Finland, in fact, resembles that of northern Minnesota, the "Land of 10,000 Lakes." There are thousands of lakes in both locations, and it is not surprising that many Finns who left their country for the United States settled in Minnesota. Compared to the size of the North American Great Lakes, which are also of glacial origin, European lakes are much smaller.

Alpine glaciers also exist in high mountain regions. As these high-elevation ice masses "flow" downslope, they scour large "U"-shaped valleys. In places such as Switzerland, southern Germany, and northern Italy, deeply scoured glacial trenches filled with water become scenic glacial lakes. Elsewhere, such as along the Norwegian coast, glaciation has created a spectacular landscape feature called "fjords." Here, glaciers that slid into the Atlantic Ocean carved hundreds of long, narrow, deep inlets that allow an arm of the sea to reach inland. Norway was ideally suited to the creation of fjords because of its poleward latitude and the Kjölen Mountains that border the North Sea coast. Fjords appear in a few locations outside of Scandinavia. The southernmost European fjord, in Montenegro, was formed by an ice-age glacier that slid into the Adriatic Sea from the Dinaric Alps.

NATURAL HAZARDS AND ENVIRONMENTAL PRESERVATION

Europe, like other regions, battles a variety of natural hazards. Earthquakes in the Mediterranean can be devastating. During warm summer months, raging fires often ravage the countryside. This is particularly true in the Mediterranean region, which extends from Portugal to Greece, because this area experiences severe summer drought. Such conflagrations destroy woodlands, Mediterranean *maquis* (scrub), agricultural land, and settlements and cause tremendous economic damage.

Floods are the most serious natural hazard in Europe. Spring rains and melting snow can send water spilling over riverbanks and into adjacent settled areas as a raging torrent. Frequent flooding is particularly severe in densely populated and highly urbanized Central and Western Europe. The Rhine River floods on an almost annual basis in Germany. Often, entire cities are under several feet of water, which limits regular functioning of communities and causes incredible property damage.

Some geographers argue that "natural" disasters should be defined as essentially "cultural" disasters because humans choose to live in potentially disastrous areas. They argue that it is not a case of nature striking out against humans; rather, it is humans taking a risk with nature. Living on the riverbanks means experiencing repeated flooding. Still, people are willing to sacrifice security for location, whether it is a picturesque coastal community in Europe or a California city located on or near the San Andreas Fault.

Europeans have invested heavily in protecting their natural environment. Only an affluent society can enjoy the costly luxury of a clean environment. Garbage and sewage disposal, reduction of industrial pollution, and preservation of pristine environments is an expensive business. European Union countries, in particular, have been reducing pollution. They also are working on legislation that will further improve environmental quality. European Union countries have implemented the Kyoto Protocol, thereby agreeing to lower the amount of carbon dioxide released into the atmosphere to 5 percent less than the 1990 level. Such actions help in many ways; one is the preservation of Central European forests that have been seriously exposed to acid rain (rainfall filled with the chemicals released by industry). Because of urbanization, agriculture, and acid rain, European forests are rapidly disappearing. Three centuries ago, one could enter the forest in Spain and walk all the way to Russia without ever leaving woodland. Today, in much of Europe, excluding Scandinavia, forests are limited and survive only in protected areas.

Europe is a relatively small area, yet within its borders the region has environmental diversity that rivals its better-known diversity of cultures. Of greatest importance, perhaps, is that most of the land is productive. Whether vineyards in France, spectacular scenery in Switzerland, forests of Scandinavia, or sunny beaches in Spain, Europe's natural environment offers something for everyone.

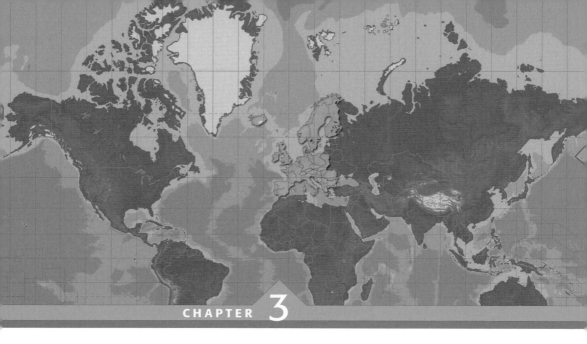

CHAPTER 3

Historical Geography

THE EARLIEST EUROPEANS

According to cultural anthropologists, culture—and thus humankind—began with the first use of language. When that happened
is not clear. It is clear that our ancestors were physically present and
roaming the land long before they used articulate language. The
earliest human presence on the European continent dates back
hundreds of thousands of years. Neanderthals, successful hunters
who lived in small groups, inhabited Western Europe before *Homo
sapiens* decided to leave Africa and cross to Asia and Europe. Scientists have shown that Neanderthals were not a different species from
Homo sapiens. Rather, they were a branch of *Homo sapiens*—like
cousins. Had they survived, Neanderthals would perhaps be sharing

the world with us and enjoying all the cultural benefits of the modern world. Today, however, we know them only through archeological research on numerous Western European caves. No one really knows what caused Neanderthals' extinction. There is some speculation that they may have been driven to extinction by stronger *Homo sapiens* who invaded their territory, but there is another theory that they simply joined *Homo sapiens* and eventually disappeared as a separate strain.

The evidence of Neanderthals' presence is particularly evident in western and southern parts of Europe, just south of the continental glaciers' southern reach. The name "Neanderthal" originated from the Neander Thal (Neander Valley) in southern Germany, where some of the first remains were found. Caves, scattered from France and Spain to Croatia, have provided many more remains and further evidence of the Neanderthals' lifestyle. For thousands of years, during the latter part of the Pleistocene ice age, these skilled hunters were the dominant humans in Europe. Toward the end of the Pleistocene, however, they were unable to resist the *Homo sapiens*' expansion. *Homo sapiens* ultimately replaced the original cavemen. The term *caveman* does not mean that all people of that time lived in caves. Caves provide a sheltered environment in which human remains and artifacts were concentrated in large numbers and protected from the elements. As a result, caves can be gold mines for archaeologists, who are able to find and analyze remains that have been preserved for thousands of years.

PRE-GREEK HUMANS

Perhaps the single most important development in human history, other than gaining control of fire, was the domestication of plants and animals. This development, called the Agricultural Revolution, had its origin perhaps 12,000 to 15,000 years ago. Many scientists believe that it originated in

Southwest Asia and gradually diffused (spread) from there to much of the known world. This was a crucial time for hunters and gatherers because they suddenly found themselves in a position to establish permanent settlements. This step eventually led to the dawn of civilizations, the most important of which were in the Mesopotamian region: Sumer, Babylon, and Assyria. This is why we refer to Mesopotamia as the "cradle of Western Civilization."

Much of what is "European" today in terms of culture traits began in the Middle East and then gradually diffused westward into Europe. Culture traits including mathematics, abstract writing, astronomy, technology, and domesticated plants and animals spread first into the Aegean world of the Ancient Greeks. Later, the spread continued to the Apennine Peninsula and Rome.

Until the Ancient Greeks established their civilization, which involved numerous small city-states, vast areas of Europe were inhabited by small wandering tribal groups. These groups had little influence on what was to become modern-day European culture. Perhaps the most important relics of the ancient pre-Greek and pre-Roman times are rock structures whose purpose remains a mystery. Such structures exist all over Western Europe; Stonehenge, in southern England, is the best known. Scientists continually speculate about the purpose and meaning of these sites. Many believe that they were erected for religious ceremonies, but why they were built is no more certain than when they were built. It is generally believed that Stonehenge-like structures date back to about 3000 B.C.

During the second millennium B.C., the only recognized civilization in Europe developed on the island of Crete. The Minoan civilization, as it is called, reached its zenith in about 1600 B.C. It soon fell into decline, however, perhaps because of natural disasters such as the violent eruption of the nearby volcanic island of Thera, also known as Santorini.

The ancient Stonehenge on Salisbury Plain was built between 3000 B.C. and 1000 B.C. Its axis aligns at the summer solstice; some scientists debate that it may have been an observatory, while many experts believe it to have simply been a place of worship.

THE CLASSICAL PERIOD AND THE ROMAN EMPIRE

Migrations trigger events that result in radical changes. The first recorded migration occurred in about 1100 B.C. This event, mentioned in the Bible as the invasion of the People of the Sea, brought various Greek tribes south into the realm of the Aegean world. With more people sharing a limited amount of available land for cultivation, colonization of the Mediterranean by those less fortunate seemed to be a good idea. During the next several hundred years, the Ancient Greeks established numerous colonies. They expanded their culture throughout the Mediterranean Sea and northward to the Black Sea. The high point of Ancient Greek colonization was between the eighth and sixth centuries B.C. In many respects, this was the beginning of Western Civilization as it is recognized today.

The Ancient Greeks both created and spread many cultural traits that represent the basis of our society: democracy, philosophy, architecture, art, sporting events, and so forth. The Summer Olympic Games, the sporting event held every four years to gather the world's best athletes, is a modern version of the event first organized in Greece in 776 B.C. Democracy, the ruling system created in Greece's city-states, is the essential element of the political structure we call the Western democratic state, like the United States. We cherish democracy and protect it when needed, even fighting wars in its defense.

The Roman Empire, which followed the Ancient Greeks, can be called the first global civilization. In almost every aspect, Rome's vast empire was more culturally dominant in Europe than any other before or after it. It lasted for an entire millennium. Within Europe, it spanned an area that extended from present-day Portugal to the shores of Turkey and northward as far as the British Isles. Organized as a military unit, the Roman Empire developed what at the time was the world's best transportation network. It connected all provinces, regardless of how remote, with Rome. (Have you heard the expression "All roads lead to Rome"?) The linkages made possible the rapid transfer of troops and goods which, in turn, allowed Rome to maintain control of the empire.

Eventually, many non-Romans developed a sense of "belonging" to the Empire. Astonishingly, the Romans were able to do what the European Union is having difficulty accomplishing: convincing Europeans that they can benefit from all belonging to one united political (and perhaps cultural) sphere! Achieving widespread integration into the empire was one of the Romans' most successful endeavors. The Eastern Roman (incorrectly called "Byzantine") Empire survived about 1,000 years after the western part of the empire by using similar principles.

Romans built the first genuine global empire, and, as in the case of the Greeks, their legacy is still visible in many ways: Most European countries have based their modern judicial systems on Roman law; the language, Latin, is very much alive in scientific and academic circles; and Roman Catholicism is the world's most influential religion. Rome itself was the first European city to have one million inhabitants.

THE MIDDLE AGES

The second major movement of people in Europe occurred between the fifth and seventh centuries A.D. As had occurred in the past, the migration created drastic cultural changes. The age of the Roman Empire was over, and the period known as the Middle Ages was fast approaching. This period of cultural decline was also known as the Dark Ages of European history, although mostly for unjustified reasons. This term is used to describe the time between the fall of the Roman Empire (A.D. 476) and the emergence of the Renaissance in the fifteenth and sixteenth centuries. The term *Dark Ages* is a product of the Renaissance intellectuals' general dislike of the Middle Ages.

Many factors, not just the established Church, as some historians assert, contributed to the period of decline. Germanic and Slavic tribes began to disrupt Roman linkages and trade routes. Eventually, these "barbarians" spilled across the Danube and began to settle in Roman-held lands, further disrupting regional stability. These events brought about major cultural changes in the region. Sophisticated urban Roman culture began to be challenged by the more traditional ways of life cherished by mostly rural invading tribal peoples. Eventually, Rome fell and its empire crumbled. Although the invaders gradually accepted some traits of Roman culture, such as Christianity, it took centuries for Europe to revive. When a cultural region undergoes major changes, the experience is much like a boxer receiving a hard blow to the stomach: It takes some time to catch a breath and recover from the shock. Medieval Europe needed just that—time to recover. The soon-to-occur Renaissance and the Age of Discovery did not suddenly happen: Both were the continuation of something. Culture builds layer on layer, both from independent innovation and by gaining traits through the process of cultural diffusion.

Consolidation of Western Europe began with the expansion of the Franks' kingdom. These Germanic tribesmen were able to gain control over most of what previously had been the Western Roman Empire. Much of their success was the result of cultural adaptation; that is, they were a Germanic tribe that accepted many Roman cultural traits. The Franks' core was in present-day France. From this area, they expanded their control throughout Western Europe, reaching Austria and the Adriatic Sea. One needs to go no farther than France today to see the results of cultural adaptation. Even though we think of the French as the epitome of Roman-based nations and culture, most residents of France have Germanic roots.

During medieval times, the Roman Catholic Church's influence in all aspects of life did not suddenly appear. Much of the Church's strength resulted from an understanding that secular rulers and clergy could mutually benefit from each other's actions. The Church's policy was that the pope is God's representative on Earth and therefore must rule over all people. Secular rulers thirsted for power and recognized the importance of having Rome on their side; therefore, they created various alliances with popes and other Church officials. Separation of church and state did not exist in Europe during the Middle Ages, especially for ordinary people. (This tradition is one reason many Europeans still have a rather negative opinion of the Roman Catholic Church.)

Despite the negative things that happened during the Middle Ages, not all life in Europe was "dark." In some respects, culture continued to flourish and even grow, although with strong religious ties. Many cities were growing, trade and transportation networks were expanding, and Gothic cathedrals reached skyward. There were measurable improvements in medieval customs, art, and everyday life for most ordinary people.

At the time of the Crusades, Europe caught its breath and was ready to begin the offensive. In 1092, Pope Urban II called for Christians to free Christ's grave in Jerusalem. These attempts, called the Crusades, lasted for two centuries and gave Europeans a glimpse of another world. It is probable that the opening of this door ultimately led to the Age of Discovery. The Age of Discovery in turn made possible the spread of European culture, political influence, and trade throughout much of the globe. Interaction with the Muslim world was significant in terms of the exchange of cultural traits. The Church called for the Crusades to expand its reach, yet ultimately they left the Church weakened. Culturally, however, European society benefited from the Crusades. This was particularly obvious in the Apennine Peninsula (Italy), where the Renaissance originated and from which it diffused throughout much of Europe.

Not every cultural interaction brings positive results. Just as Europeans introduced various diseases to Native Americans, thereby destroying entire tribes, medieval Europe experienced tremendous difficulties with diseases transferred from Asia. One of the most devastating episodes in European history was the epidemic of bubonic plague during the 1340s. Almost 20 million people—one-third of Europe's population—died in this scourge. The bacterium, transferred by rats that lived on the ships that sailed between Asia and Europe, spread quickly through the continent. Only parts of Poland escaped the epidemic. Growing urban areas with a higher concentration of people accelerated the spread of the disease, as did the lack of clean water and personal hygiene. In such conditions, it is difficult to prevent epidemics, especially in a time when vaccines had not yet been developed. Europeans survived the old-fashioned way, with genetic resistance. On average, one of eight persons is immune to the plague, whereas seven of eight will die if infected. By natural selection, the surviving person's descendants will become immune to the plague because of their ancestors' resistance. Genetics saved European culture.

THE RENAISSANCE AND THE AGE OF DISCOVERY

The fifteenth and sixteenth centuries brought numerous changes to Europe, which rapidly became the "center of the world." Technological improvements set a path for developments in education, architecture, art, political institutions, trade, and so forth. Johann Gutenberg's invention of movable type in the mid-fifteenth century revolutionized printing and knowledge exchange. People no longer were limited to reading only religious and Church-approved handwritten texts. The impact of this change is clearly illustrated in the success of the sixteenth-century Protestant Reformation, led by Martin Luther. Martin Luther's writings reached readers in a short period of time and kept them informed of current events.

Improvements in navigation allowed mariners to extend voyages far beyond European shores. Although Christopher Columbus discovered the Americas in 1492 for the Spanish crown, the real pioneers of navigation were the Portuguese. Under the leadership of Henry the Navigator, the Portuguese explored the African coastal waters during the fifteenth century. These explorations opened the road for Columbus. Many other

explorers followed, including Ferdinand Magellan, whose ships circumnavigated the world in the 1520s. Magellan was killed in a fight with natives in the Philippines and did not complete the voyage himself. Later, British, French, and Dutch explorers became involved in the European voyages of discovery.

Sixteenth-century Europe, although developing quickly, was hardly a peaceful place to reside. The Roman Catholic Church was losing its dominance, and various Protestant factions—Lutherans, Calvinists, and others—were gaining ground. Religious conflict led to burning antagonism, excommunication, and war. At the same time, the Ottoman (Osman) Turks kept Southeastern Europe under siege. From a small tribe that wandered Asia Minor, they increased in power to levels rarely seen before. They created a large empire, replacing the remains of the Eastern Roman Empire. Their control and strong cultural influence over many European nations, particularly in the southeast, lasted for more than four centuries and in some areas until World War I. Even today, numerous cultural traits of Turkish origin are present among Bulgarians, Greeks, Serbs, Bosnians, and Macedonians. This is especially true in regard to customs and traditions.

STEPS TOWARD MODERN EUROPE

The European culture region began to restructure in the seventeenth century. The first nation–states (one nationality of people who are self-governing) began to emerge. Leadership was by absolute rulers, such as Louis XIV in France. This was the beginning of a process that culminated in the nineteenth century. It was a time of strong positive nationalism and the search for freedom through independence movements for many nations. During the reign of Louis XIV (1643–1715), France became one of the most influential countries in the world. The French lifestyle spread among members of the European high class, and the French language became the main medium of communication among people of different cultural backgrounds (today,

English, fills a similar role in global communication). Rulers of many other countries sought to implement the governing methods employed by Louis XIV. He ruled by absolute and un-questioned power.

In about the same period, the bourgeoisie began to rise in influence. This middle-class, city-based social group eventually led Europe toward one of the largest cultural changes in history: the Industrial Revolution. The principle of steam power, or simple steam engines, had been around for centuries. By the late eighteenth century, it had developed into a very important source of power. Its use in powering railway and ship engines, as well as in other areas, triggered a tremendous leap forward in cultural development. It immediately elevated Europe to the role of the world's leading superpower in nearly all aspects of life. As the industrial economy grew, capital was available for many other things. Cities grew and with them rail and shipping networks. The advent of formal education (including colleges), advances in medicine, and other developments propelled the standard of living forward at an unprecedented rate.

The Industrial Revolution's impact on world culture can be compared only with that of the Agricultural Revolution thousands of years earlier. It changed the lifestyles of millions, and ultimately billions, of people. Society was rapidly transformed from the slow-paced and very traditional rural folk culture to the fast-changing popular culture associated with urban life. The European cultural landscape was drastically changed as well. This was particularly obvious in the industrial centers of Great Britain. There, coal-smoke–belching chimneys, filthy streets, and endless rows of dismal brick housing symbolized progress. These conditions may not seem like progress, but they were the beginning of the prosperity that the industrial world enjoys today.

The latter half of the nineteenth century and the first part of the twentieth century also saw the age of colonialism. European powers such as the United Kingdom, France, the Netherlands, Belgium, and Italy colonized and controlled large portions of

the African and Asian continents. The process mainly involved the exercise of European power and influence and a huge drain on the resources (natural, agricultural, and human) of the lands that were colonized. Colonization also was significant in a cultural sense. Millions of people worldwide had contact with the European culture, and the results of this contact are particularly visible in many contemporary African countries. A colonial tongue, such as English or French, is the official language, European religions are practiced by native peoples, and aspects of the colonial legacy still represent a major part of local lifestyle.

Recent decades have brought yet another challenge to the European culture region—unification under the umbrella of the European Union. How this development, which is still in progress, will play out and what effects it will have on transforming the continent remain to be seen. A fully united Europe could very easily become the world's leading power. Stay tuned! History may again be in the making with Europe as the focal point.

</br>

CHAPTER **4**

Population Geography

Population conditions and trends are generally the result of economic development. In the case of Europe, demographic (population) changes began to occur with the onset of the Industrial Revolution in the nineteenth century and continue today. With the dawn of the industrial age, population distribution followed a general shift from rural to urban. This trend began in the United Kingdom and spread to France. People began to gather in booming cities, resulting in urban clusters of high population density. Initially, fertility rates (the number of children to which a woman gives birth) rose dramatically. People began to speak of a "population explosion" and the dire consequences of "over-population."

</br>

More than a century later, Europe's demographic picture has changed again. Today, the region is experiencing a rapid decrease in fertility rates. In many countries and within the region as a whole, population is declining. In fact, the region's low reproduction rates are now considered a cultural problem of major proportion. Some observers even warn that Europeans, and with them much of their culture, may die out—although this would not happen for some time. Of greater short-term concern is Europe's rapidly aging population. How can a society support a growing population of citizens who are beyond their (economically) productive years? Western Europe, in particular, has entered what geographers refer to as a "postindustrial phase." This means that people are engaged in things such as information processing, services, or some other nonindustrial activity. Postindustrialism creates a unique set of demographic conditions shared by most developed countries.

This chapter discusses traditional population issues with emphasis on cultural, rather than statistical, aspects. Several important factors, including industrialization, education, urbanization, emigration, population decline, and the consequences of a declining and aging population, are addressed.

AN AGING CONTINENT

Patterns of population growth generally follow predictable norms unless interrupted by an extraordinary event such as war, famine, or epidemic. Nearly all cultures pass from a stage of slow population growth to one of very rapid growth and then to slow growth again. This is called the "demographic transition." Stages of the transition are agricultural (slow growth), industrial (rapid growth), and postindustrial (slow growth). Until the nineteenth century, agriculture was the predominant economic activity of most Europeans. Population density was low, with scattered, small urban centers. Only certain cities, such as London and Paris, had significant populations. Before the revolution of 1789, France was Europe's most populated country.

The rapidly aging population is a short-term concern for Europeans. Many areas, including Western Europe, have entered a postindustrial phase, which is a time of slow population growth.

Rural families traditionally have much higher birthrates than do urban couples, but life expectancy in preindustrial Europe was short. Medical advancements were slow to reach the countryside, and infant mortality was very high. It was not uncommon for a woman to give birth to as many as 20 children, but perhaps only one-third of them survived to adulthood. In rural environments, children are a capital resource: They can perform work.

This is not the permanent case in most cities. When rapid industrialization happened, first in the United Kingdom and later elsewhere, the demand for a work force drastically in-

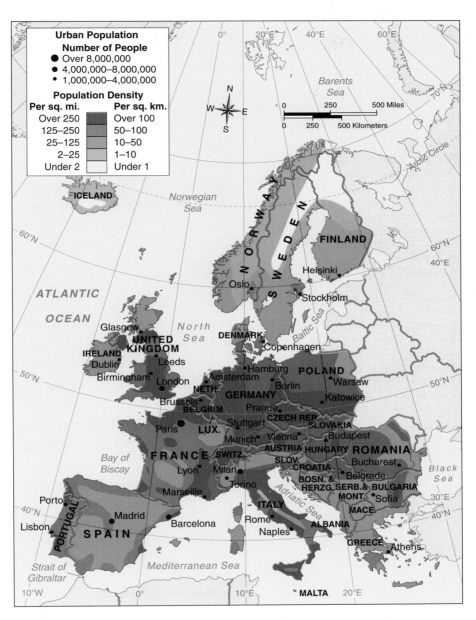

Urban Population
Number of People
- Over 8,000,000
- 4,000,000–8,000,000
- 1,000,000–4,000,000

Population Density

Per sq. mi.	Per sq. km.
Over 250	Over 100
125–250	50–100
25–125	10–50
2–25	1–10
Under 2	Under 1

This is a population map of Europe. Parts of Germany, France, and Italy still remain the most populated areas per square mile.

creased. Birth rates remained high, and for a variety of reasons—medical advances, improvements in agricultural production, and an awareness of hygiene—mortality (death) rates declined. France, which entered industrialization several decades after other countries, fell behind in population. At the beginning of the nineteenth century France's population was almost three times higher than that of the United Kingdom. By the beginning of the twentieth century, both countries were equal. Everywhere in Europe, the picture was similar. Contemporary Italy has about 60 million residents and the fifth-largest economy in the world. Its population (and economic) growth was minor, however, until industrialization began to increase, which happened after World War I. Although the demographic transition affects all areas, it certainly does not affect them at the same time. The process of diffusion often requires considerable time for cultural traits to spread from their point of origin elsewhere. In Europe, it happened gradually from country to country. It is important to remember that population growth or decline must be regarded as a cultural process, because humans determine population dynamics.

Ironically, although the Industrial Revolution provided Europeans (and humankind, for that matter) with unprecedented economic growth, it was also the key to reducing population growth. This occurred for a number of reasons. There was a sharp increase in formal education, including that of women. Personal freedom expanded, as did economic opportunities. Raising children in the city is more costly than doing so in the country, and unlike in rural life, urban youngsters rarely contribute to family income. As a result of these and other factors, in most industrialized European countries, the rate of population increase began to drop. Today, in most of Europe, the rate of fertility decline is gaining momentum.

The connection among women, formal education, and birthrates is easily explained. The relationship can be illustrated with two sharply contrasting examples: ethnic Albanians in

Rural areas in much of Europe are less well developed than are the region's urban environments.

Albania and the former Yugoslavia, and urban residents of once-Communist Eastern European countries. Northern Albania is the poorest part of Europe. It is mired in the past: Tribal laws still represent the ultimate authority. In many ways, life there is reminiscent of the medieval lifestyle. One of the major characteristics of this lifestyle is a strong patriarchal (male-dominated) society. In this system, the rights of women are extremely limited; their role in society is to bear children and work around the house. The husband rules home and family with an iron fist. In this social environment, women are not allowed to make independent decisions. Their situation is much like that of most women throughout all of Europe a century or more ago. Not surprisingly, Albania has the highest rate of natural population increase in Europe. Its population is also Europe's youngest.

In Eastern European countries formerly under Communist rule, conditions are quite different. In fact, by 2004, every country in this region was experiencing a negative rate of natural increase—they were losing population. At the same time, citizens of these countries are visibly "aging," with more people older than 50 than younger than 15. Except for countries of former Yugoslavia, where demographics were distorted by the ethnic conflicts in the 1990s, the answer for the current population trend in Eastern Europe is simple: The region's former Communist governments industrialized and urbanized the countries. They also ensured that everyone, regardless of gender, received an education and adequate health care. After World War II, the rural-to-urban ratio shifted rapidly to favor the urban. The rate of formal education of females increased rapidly, and as educated women decided to pursue professional careers in a cash economy, the fertility rate eventually began to drop rapidly. The results in terms of population growth were identical to those that occurred in Western Europe.

The consequences of a declining and aging population in Europe are many, but economic difficulties are of greatest concern. There are not enough young people in or entering the work force to support further economic development, and social services must be provided for a rapidly growing number of retirees. As people age, much greater demands are made on increasingly costly health and medical care facilities. Many European countries see migration as the answer to their growing population dilemma.

MIGRATION

Europe has experienced two major waves of migration and, as many in the European Union believe, is on the brink of a third. The first massive migration, perhaps as many as 50 million, was to the New World—the Americas and Australia—over a period of several centuries. The second, during the second half of the twentieth century, involved numerous migrations among countries within the European culture region itself and from former colonies to France and the United Kingdom in particular. Finally, with the current expansion of the European Union eastward, migration from poorer areas of Eastern Europe toward the richer areas of Western Europe is expected to occur.

During the nineteenth century and first half of the twentieth century, Europe underwent a huge loss of people. They left their homelands in pursuit of a better life elsewhere. In several stages, disenfranchised masses of British, Irish, Scandinavians, and Germans left, mainly for North America. They were followed by waves of Italians, Greeks, and Slavs. In terms of numbers, ethnic Germans were the largest group of European emigrants. In the United States today, a majority of the population claims German ancestry. Not all Germans came from the present-day country of Germany, however: Many emigrated from the Habsburg Empire (Austria-Hungary), Poland, or Russia—countries where ethnic Germans lived for generations.

Emigration left some countries weakened. In Ireland, for example, the great potato famine of the 1840s triggered an unprecedented wave of departures. More than one million people left Ireland in a period of just five years. It has been claimed that, today, ten times as many persons with Irish ancestry live outside of Ireland than in that country. Approximately one-third of all ethnic Italians reside outside of Italy, with a majority of them in the United States.

Post-World War II migrations resulted from both choice and force. Germans and Germany played a major role in this situation as well. After the defeat of Nazi Germany, millions of ethnic Germans freely left or were forced to leave Eastern

Europe, especially Poland and Czechoslovakia. A huge loss of life in the war also left Germany without the work force needed for reconstruction; therefore, the government invited foreign workers, given temporary work permits, to help rebuild the country. Millions of Southeastern Europeans responded to this opportunity. History has shown that "temporary" visits rarely end and often become permanent. Today, Germany is home to several million Turks, Greeks, Italians, and various groups from the former Yugoslavia. Switzerland's need for a work force led to rapid immigration, some legal and some illegal. Today, almost 20 percent of the country's population of 7.2 million is foreign born. This is a major political issue for those who feel uneasy about the presence of such a high number of non-natives. Other countries, primarily former colonial powers such as the United Kingdom, France, and the Netherlands, also have significant numbers of migrants from their former African, Asian, and Caribbean colonies.

Recently, with the rapid eastward expansion of the European Union, many in Western Europe have raised concerns that the ethnic and demographic picture of Europe will change once again. In 2004, the European Union accepted ten new members, almost all former Communist-bloc countries of Eastern Europe and the former Soviet Union. A huge economic gap exists between Western Europe and Eastern Europe. With the elimination of political boundaries, people are now free to move about as they like. As a result, millions of impoverished people in Eastern Europe are beginning to look westward for a better future. Perhaps the fears of many Western Europeans are unwarranted. When Spain and Portugal were accepted into the European Union during the 1980s, there was widespread fear that these Iberians would swamp the countries of Northwestern Europe in search of employment. This proved not to be the case. In fact, greater numbers of Spanish and Portuguese began to return to their homelands than those leaving the countries.

War can cause huge changes in populations. Millions of people lost their lives in World Wars I and II, and huge areas were left in ruin. During the 1990s, there were various conflicts in the territory of former Yugoslavia. Hundreds of thousands of people were killed, and millions left their homeland. Bosnia and Herzegovina was hit the hardest, with more than 250,000 killed and more than one million displaced. This loss was a huge blow to a country with a population of a little less than four million.

IS EUROPE OVERPOPULATED?

Europe's population density is exceeded only by that of Asia. This poses the question of whether the continent is suffering from overpopulation. Many people believe that population density, which leads to crowding, is the primary factor that indicates a condition of overpopulation. By placing the emphasis on numbers of people, however, they overlook the all-important cultural factor. What density of population determines a condition of overpopulation—is it 10, 100, or 1,000 per square mile? There is no number or density that defines overpopulation. If population density were used as the only indicator of overpopulation, then Monaco, San Marino, and Liechtenstein would rank among the world's most overpopulated countries. These are some of the world's most affluent, best-educated, and long-living homelands! At the other extreme, some countries in arid North Africa have fewer than ten people per square mile (six per square kilometer) and poverty is widespread, few people are educated, and life spans are short.

The answer to the question is "No." Europe is not overpopulated. Most European countries have a high population, a high population density, and huge cities, but only the North American culture realm exceeds Europe's per capita gross national product (GNP). People are attracted to places where they can find good jobs and enjoy a high standard of living with plenti-

Industrial cities in Europe, such as London, have grown immensely since the nineteenth century. The cause of this growth can be tied to economic success and higher standards of living.

ful educational opportunities and medical care. Large cities are usually centers of economic growth and other opportunities. In fact, such cities grew because of their economic success. London and Paris for example, grew as industrial cities, and in the early nineteenth century, both surpassed a population of one million.

Throughout nearly all of Europe, many more people are urban dwellers than rural dwellers. Even in Poland, a country with an emerging economy where farming still is an important contributor to the national economy, 64 percent of residents live in cities. In the Netherlands, only 11 percent of the population is rural. Europe's current population trends, including the decrease in natural population rate, will continue. As a result, the population will continue to age. This aging population will perhaps result in a continuation of east-to-west migration by people seeking to fill the jobs vacated by the aging population.

CHAPTER 5

Culture and Society

You are now familiar with the European culture region's physical characteristics, culture history, and population trends. In this chapter, you will learn about the contemporary way of life in Europe. Emphasis is placed on ethnicity, religion, nationality, language, and social relations among the region's individuals and ethnic groups. Health, customs, and cuisine (diet) are included as well. Food is addressed because many geographers agree that diet and foodways form one of the most important traits of any culture.

ETHNIC MAKEUP

At a time during which Europe is rapidly becoming economically and politically integrated, it is easy to forget about the tremendous cultural complexity that characterizes this region of the world. Soon, political maps will not show a politically fragmented territory with dozens of different countries, some larger than many U.S. states and others smaller than Rhode Island. Political maps can, but often do not, show a region's ethnic makeup, and political boundaries rarely follow simple logic and common sense. Because of a long history and numerous migrations, Europe's ethnic map is extremely colorful. Some colors cover large areas of territory, such as those that indicate Germans or French. Others, like the Roma (Gypsies), are acknowledged only with dots or footnotes because of lesser and widely scattered representation.

The culture region's ethnic structure is mainly composed of three major groups: Germanic, Slavic, and Romanic, each of which branches into numerous smaller groups. There are other people who do not belong to any of these groups, and in some locations, they are present in significant numbers.

Germanic Peoples

Germanic stock includes Germans, Swedes, Norwegians, Danes, Dutch (Flemish), and English (Anglo-Saxon). Germanic people are the descendants of the original tribes that wandered Central and Eastern Europe during the time of the Roman Empire. Their migration was influenced by the Huns, who stormed out of Central Asia and pillaged everything in their path. To escape the wrath of the Huns, the Germanic tribes moved westward and southward across the Danube and into the Roman Empire. Once there, they established permanent settlements and quickly brought about the end of this once vast and powerful empire.

Not all Germanic tribes survived through the centuries. The word *vandal* comes from a tribe of the same name that was known among Romans for the massive destruction it caused to life and property within their empire. Vandals eventually settled in North Africa but soon disappeared from history's stage.

Other tribes, such as the Franks, accepted the Roman culture and became the French nation. Today, people of Germanic descent live mostly in Central and Northern Europe.

Slavic Peoples

People of Slavic stock reside in the east, where they extend into Russia and Ukraine, Europe's two largest countries. Slavs are divided into three groups: Eastern (Russians, Belorussians, and Ukrainians), Western (Poles, Czechs, Slovakians, and Luzice Serbs), and Southern (Slovenes, Croats, Serbs, Bosnian Muslims (Bosniaks), Montenegrins, Macedonians, and Bulgarians). For the purpose of this book, Eastern Slavs are excluded from the European culture region. Slavic tribes, like the Germanic peoples, originally roamed the steppes between present-day Poland and Eastern Ukraine. They finally settled throughout Eastern, Central, and Southeastern Europe. Bulgarians, like the Franks in France, were of different stock (Turkish-Mongolian) and smaller numbers (20,000) than the native population, but they were powerful enough to conquer the local Slavic population, giving them their name.

The Southern Slavic group is perhaps the most difficult for Americans to fully comprehend. Similarities exist in language and many customs, yet people are divided by ethnicity, which in this case is a political creation. For a number of years, all Southern Slavs have lived in just two countries, Bulgaria and Yugoslavia (which means "a country of the South Slavs"). With the breakup of Yugoslavia in 1991, several new countries were created; they politically divided people of similar culture who spoke the same language. Bosniaks, for example, differed from neighboring Croats and Serbs only in terms of their respective religions, but that religion was used as a basis for the creation of a new ethnicity: In the 1970s, the Yugoslav government granted the Muslim religious group the status of an ethnic group with certain political rights. Twenty years later, the Muslims came to be called "Bosniaks" in recognition of their ethnic difference from Serbs and Croats.

Romanic Peoples

People of Romanic stock are Portuguese, Spaniards, French, Belgian Walloons, Italians, Romanians, and Moldavians. Their most prominent common characteristic is that of Latin language roots and, except in the case of the last two, west Mediterranean location. Looking at a map of the Roman Empire reveals the cultural "reach" that locked the western Mediterranean into the everlasting Romanic sphere.

Other Ethnic Groups

Several other European nations do not belong to any of the three major groups. There are the Albanians, who are descendants of the ancient Illyrians. At one point, they lived throughout most of Southeastern Europe. Today, they reside in their ethnic homeland, Albania, and in several neighboring countries, including Serbia and Montenegro, Greece, and Macedonia.

Another ancient people, the Basques, consider the borderland between northwestern Spain and southwestern France their homeland. Basques are known for vigorously preserving their ethnic identity, even at the price of armed conflict against the Spanish government.

Although they look European, Hungarians and Finns are originally of Asian stock and are Uralic-Altaic people, cousins to Turks and Central Asians. They migrated into their present homelands during medieval times.

Celtic peoples live mainly on the British Isles. At one time, Celtic tribes lived from the Baltic Sea southward to the Mediterranean shores. Today, their descendents are known as the Irish, Scots, Welsh, and Cornish, in Ireland and on the British Isles, and as the Bretons in western France.

Greeks have been living along the shores of the Aegean Sea for more than 3,000 years. They were the great colonizers of the Mediterranean world who controlled lands from the Iberian Peninsula to the eastern shores of the Black Sea. Today, the majority of Greeks reside within the country that bears their name.

Gypsies, or Roma, as they call themselves, are a remarkable ethnic group. They are believed to have originated in India. From there, beginning in the fourteenth century, they drifted westward into Europe. Roma have clung to many of their ancient customs and traditions. They represent significant minorities in several countries including Slovakia, Hungary, Romania, and Serbia and Montenegro.

Southeastern Europe is home to many Turks as well. A majority of them live in Turkey, but many ethnic Turks live in other neighboring countries of the so-called Balkan Peninsula. As noted previously, Turks are of Altaic origin (Altai is a mountain range between Russia, Kazakhstan, and Mongolia).

To list and adequately describe all of Europe's ethnic groups would take a separate book. Throughout the region, there are countless more ethnicities than are listed here, some of which number only a few thousand. In some respects, present-day Europe is much like the United States. Europe, however, is a geographic region with much greater cultural diversity than the United States. In a matter of hours, one can pass through half a dozen cultural transitions every bit as great as the one that exists between the United States and Mexico or between New England and French Quebec. The great cultural complexity can be illustrated by Kosovo, a region with an area comparable to that of Connecticut. During the 1990s, political leaders were searching for a political solution to the "Kosovo problem." Ignorant of the region's cultural complexity, the politicians thought that only Albanians and Serbs live there. They worked to create the best solution for the region based on these two ethnicities—until they were informed that about 24 different ethnic groups called Kosovo home!

LANGUAGE

After learning about Europe's ethnicity, it is much easier to understand the region's linguistic structure. Language almost always coincides with ethnic boundaries. That is to say, language binds most (although not all) ethnic groups together. Despite the great differences between them, most European languages have a common source. They came out of southwestern Asia perhaps as long as 10,000 years ago. From there, the language gradually spread as people migrated eastward to India and westward to Europe (hence its name: Indo-European language family).

As language spread over the millennia, groups became separated from one another. Eventually, the language they spoke evolved into different branches that share a common root. As a result, the Indo-European linguistic family has grown to include dozens of related tongues. Germanic, Slavic, and Romanic languages all share the same roots, and many words with the same meaning sound similar in all three language groups. This is especially true for words that identify common, yet important, things such as water or salt.

The Greek, Albanian, and Celtic language groups are all Indo-European, but some others are not. Hungarians, for example, were one of the latest arrivals in Europe; they did not settle in their current homeland until the tenth century. They invaded from central Asia, and their language is of the Uralic-Altaic group, as is Turkish. The Finnish language also belongs to this group's Uralic (named after the Russian mountain range) branch; this language has several million speakers in the northern part of the culture region. The most mysterious of all European languages is Basque, spoken by people who live mainly in an area just to the west of the Pyrenees in northern Spain. Scientists still do not know who the Basques are, where they came from, or to whom they might be related. One theory states that they came from the Caucasus Mountains in southern Russia. Other than the fact that their language is not Indo-European, few scholars are able to agree on anything that relates to the origin of these interesting people. Even the Indian branch of Indo-European languages is significantly represented in Europe. Hundreds of thousands of Roma (Gypsy) people have preserved the tongue since they entered Europe, although it is spoken in different variations.

RELIGION

When outsiders look at Europe in search of culture traits common to all people who live in the region, religious uniformity usually tops the list. The continent seems to stand as the ultimate fortress of Christianity. This is a role it has held since the age of the Roman Empire. The perceptions of Europe being a nearly homogeneous Christian stronghold are far removed from today's reality. In fact, religious diversity there is centuries old, and different factions of Christianity have played an important role throughout the region. The assumption of a monolithic Christian grip on Europe is perhaps the product of nostalgia about the times of medieval knights and warriors fighting in the Crusades.

The religious landscape of contemporary Europe forms a fragmented picture. Northern Europe is dominantly Protestant. It was here, in the mid-sixteenth century, that Martin Luther provided the leadership that contributed to the Protestant Reformation and formation of the Lutheran faith. Throughout Northern Europe, however, and particularly in Scandinavia, society is becoming increasingly secular. Most people claim to be agnostics or atheists, and few practice religion in any form. The same holds true in the former Communist countries of Eastern Europe. There, political authorities did not favor organized religion during Communist years. As a result, most people are generally apathetic about religion and have little interest in attending church.

Throughout history, Europe has been ravaged by many religious conflicts. The clergy, particularly Roman Catholic clergy, had a very strong influence on political affairs, and this often spilled over into warfare between conflicting interests. As a result of the church's influence, some countries insisted on a complete separation of church and state. France played a leadership role in this separation. In 2004, while drafting the constitution of the European Union, France rejected any wording that included even a slight hint of religion. The country held firm that there should not even be mention of Europe's Christian heritage. To Ameri-

Although Europe has become increasingly secular, Christianity has been the region's dominant faith since Roman times. Many old churches, such as this basilica in Italy, are important tourist sites today.

cans—whose country, many believe, is founded on Christianity and whose current president often mentions God in public—this may seem rather unusual. Many Europeans are bewildered over the importance of religion in America and the frequent public displays of religious beliefs by political leaders and others.

Christian Europe is divided mainly among the Roman Catholic, the Eastern Orthodox, and Protestant (Lutheran, Anglican, and so forth) faiths. There are smaller churches, such as the Greco Catholic, which follows many Eastern Orthodox practices but recognizes the supremacy of the Roman Catholic pope. Although a majority of European Jews (up to 6 million) perished during the Holocaust and many others left for Israel, Judaism is still widely represented in urban Europe today.

Originally from the Middle East, Jews migrated to Europe in the first and second centuries after being forced by the Romans to leave their homeland in Palestine. It is important to recognize that, technically, Jews are not an ethnic group (which is why they are not mentioned in the Ethnicity section). They are differentiated on the basis of their common religion rather than on common racial or cultural ancestry. One can become Jewish by choice, as many have, by accepting Judaic principles; in contrast, one must be born into and raised as a member of an ethnic group. Geographically, European Jews are divided into two groups: Sephardic and Ashkenazi. The former generally are from the Iberian Peninsula, and the latter are from Germany, Poland, and the rest of Central Europe.

The Muslim population in Europe is growing rapidly, mainly through migration from former European colonies in Africa and Asia. France, the United Kingdom, and Germany all have several million residents of Islamic faith, a majority of them immigrants. Native peoples in Europe who practice Islam are generally limited to small populations. There are small pockets of Muslims in both Southeastern and Southwestern Europe. Only Albania has a dominantly Muslim population, with 70 percent practicing that faith.

SOCIAL RELATIONS

In terms of social relations, Europe is somewhat similar to the United States—which is, after all, a North American branch of the European culture in many ways. There are some significant differences as well. Perhaps one of the most visible differences is the European welfare state versus the American individualistic free-enterprise system. In Europe, there is strong government involvement in the lives of ordinary people in terms of social equality. Europeans see the state as an instrument for providing for the masses. Taxation is high, but health insurance and other benefits are universal. The system is designed to provide help to everyone and to not allow anyone to fall behind. As a result, most people share a similar scale (attainment versus standard which is a goal) of living. Europe has a strong tradition of unionization (collective bargaining), whereas many elements of socialism are present in traditional capitalistic societies, such as in Great Britain. A sense of security is important, and the feeling of belonging and working for a common good is, for many Europeans, a significant part of the lifestyle. This is particularly obvious in Scandinavian countries.

In the United States, the system is designed differently. People see the state as the opportunity for thriving individualism. Each person has a chance to establish and reach for the highest possible goals based on work and merit. Neither the American nor the European way is necessarily right or wrong; they simply are different. Both systems reflect the unique historical and cultural conditions under which they separately evolved.

Even the casual tourist traveling through Europe will notice that the ordinary European lifestyle is more "laid back" and easy going. More time is spent on leisure activities. The cultural landscape often reflects a preference for life at a much slower pace than is common in the United States. The convenience stores and fast-food outlets so common in the United States are replaced by small shops and meals that can last for hours. The perceived need for a stressful corporate-driven mentality is still foreign to a majority of people. In such a social environment, it is not difficult to understand why family gatherings and dining are very important even today throughout much of the European culture region.

DIET, CUISINE, AND HEALTH

A famous French gourmet once noticed that people's personalities are reflections of their dietary habits. Many agree, because more and more studies about the importance of proper diet in regard to health issues are published in medical journals. Whether people live longer because of a properly balanced diet (and active lifestyle) remains open to question. Some examples from Europe contribute to the belief that proper diet contributes

Europeans value their leisure time and enjoy dining at outdoor cafes, where they can share a meal with friends and family.

to longevity. Although famous regional cuisines such as Italian or French exist, European dietary habits are separated into two basic groups: coastal and continental.

The first group is best known through Mediterranean cuisine. Its meals generally consist of fresh seafood, legumes, herbs, red wine, and plenty of olive oil. Meat, especially red meat, is consumed rarely, perhaps once a week or only several times a month. Freshness of ingredients and low cholesterol are the keys to preventing heart disease, a leading killer in developed countries. In areas where the Mediterranean diet is widely consumed, the results are obvious. On the Greek island of Crete and other islands in the Mediterranean Sea, life expectancies tend to be much longer than elsewhere in Europe.

Continental cuisine concentrates on less fish and much more on red meat, cured and smoked pork, bread, butter, and animal fat. Although delicious, such food provides more concerns about health risks. In countries that have distinct boundaries between the two cuisines, such as boomerang-shaped Croatia, heart disease incidence is always higher in the meat-eating interior rather than the seafood-eating areas, as are the cases of obesity.

In regard to alcohol consumption, Europeans are liberal. Some countries have attempted to limit consumption by levying heavy taxes on alcohol. What constitutes "overconsumption" varies greatly and is judged by local standards. Sweden and Norway are two of the strictest. Southern Europe is most liberal, which makes sense considering its cultural history. In dominantly Catholic Southern Europe, the role of wine was always important. It is the leading alcoholic drink consumed in all European countries that border the Mediterranean Sea. Viticulture (growing of grapes, most of which are used in the making of wine) is among the leading agricultural activities. The French and others believe in wine's medical benefits, a claim supported by the discovery of the so-called French paradox in the 1970s and 1980s. According to nutritional scientists, because of the intake of red wine in particular, French people have lower rates of heart disease. This is true despite the fact that much of their cuisine is composed of high-fat foods and thus presents an automatic risk for heart disease.

Unfortunately, things are beginning to change in many parts of Europe. Proper diet, exercise, and other strong traditions are giving way to lifestyles associated with the United States. Many people now drive rather than walk or ride bicycles. A fast-food meal is now commonplace for many urbanites. This trend is rapidly spreading. Once unimaginable, obesity problems are increasing among the European population. Rates of obesity are higher for children than for adults because of less physical activity and the attraction to fast food. Although European problems are minor compared with those that confront the United States, some countries are taking positive steps to stop the trend before it becomes worse. Childhood obesity

Viticulture is one of France's main agricultural activities. The French, who drink more wine per capita than any other people, suffer relatively low rates of heart disease. Many physicians believe that wine, consumed in moderation, is good for health.

prevention programs have been implemented in Italy. Ireland was even considering implementation of a so-called fat tax to fight growing obesity, blaming fast food. Some Europeans admit that obesity prevention, and the health risks obesity raises, must be a priority of education and public awareness.

EDUCATION

Primary and secondary education in Europe are generally similar to that in the United States in terms of grade-level organization. Higher education is considerably different. European universities have always been reserved for the "best and brightest." Entrance has been limited to the relatively small percentage of those fortunate enough to pass classification exams and qualify for admission. In the United States, higher education has been much more open. Most high-school graduates are eligible to continue their education in a college, university, or technical school. The European system has turned out an elite class, whereas the United States has attempted to educate all those willing and able to pursue the further acquisition of knowledge. A primary difference is that Americans generally must pay for their education, whether outright through tuition or by subsidized scholarships. In Europe, once accepted, students usually have a "free ride" because higher education is supported through public taxes.

With the policy that limits college enrollment to only the most qualified students, European countries have been able to establish and maintain very high educational standards. In the United States, with its more lax entrance requirements, academic standards have been eroding for decades.

As a result of its restrictive admissions policy, Europe now faces the problem of what to do with the great number of people who were unable to attend college. In some countries, it has been suggested that access to higher education should be open to many more people. The suggestion that this be done with direct financing from students themselves has brought cries of outrage. Many people fear that once universities begin to function as corporate-driven institutions, as they do in the United States, academic standards and free thought will disintegrate. Once again, both the European and American systems have merit. Both evolved through time in response to the needs characteristics of the different societies.

CUSTOMS AND TRADITIONS

As should be expected, hundreds of millions of people spread across a large culture region do not all have the same customs. Customs and traditions vary from country to country and also among different groups within a country. Regional differences are perhaps the most interesting to observe. They are particularly noticeable in Southern and Southeastern Europe. Here, cultural leftovers from the contact between domestic and foreign (Turkish and Arab) influences still play a major role in the everyday lives of ordinary people. Distinct traditions are also better preserved in rural areas. In the more remote areas, many people continue to practice a folk culture—a traditional way of life relatively unchanged for generations.

In much of the region, if a person visits friends or family, it would be considered highly offensive for him or her to stay in a hotel rather than in the host's house. When visiting after an extended period of time, it is considered proper to bring small gifts, perhaps a bottle of wine. One should always offer to remove his or her shoes when entering a house in order to avoid offending the hosts. This is particularly important in Southeastern Europe, where shoe removal on entering a home was introduced by the Turks. In the Middle Eastern tradition, people usually sit on the floor covered with carpets and socialize, drink tea, and dine. Wearing shoes means bringing dirt into the home, soiling the (often extremely expensive) carpets, and contaminating areas on which people sit to eat. Even though most people sit at tables today, the tradition of removing one's shoes is strong and probably will not change soon.

In some areas of Europe, it is inappropriate to not stay for dinner while visiting, whereas in others it is exactly the opposite. Similarly, a good way to offend friends in Eastern Europe is to ask to split the bill in a restaurant, but in much of Western Europe it is completely normal and expected. A traveler can discover some amazing unwritten rules that make the joy and excitement of travel through Europe unforgettable. The author remembers traveling the continent during his teenage years. He was fortunate to meet different people of different backgrounds and learn what the word *culture* is all about. It is amazing how much one can learn about different food and music just by traveling with truck drivers!

CHAPTER 6

Political Geography

European political issues are, without a doubt, some of the most intriguing to those who have an interest in political geography. Modern political ideologies, parliamentary democracy, fascism, and Communism all originated in this cultural region. Europe survived two world wars and a half-century of the Cold War. It now is undergoing the sweeping political changes in the European Union, including expansion beyond the region's traditional boundaries.

MODERN POLITICAL HISTORY

The emergence of political institutions followed the Industrial Revolution and its accompanying rapid urbanization in the nineteenth century. These developments helped spawn a middle class that grew rapidly in power and influence. Power began to shift from a few elite individuals to the booming factory work force and urban populations. During this time, major ideologies such as liberalism and socialism appeared, in part as a result of concerns over the directions in which European society was going. This was also the time of expanding nationalism, the idea that people who share the same ancestry and language should live together in one state. (Although a noble idea for the nineteenth century, this feeling caused numerous conflicts during the twentieth century and continues to do so in some parts of the world.) In Italy and Germany, desire to have one large state rather than many small political fragments was particularly popular. The territory now occupied by these countries was, at that time, held by many small, semi-independent states, some the size of a typical U.S. county. Nationalist movements eventually prevailed, and Italy and Germany became united nation–states during the latter half of the nineteenth century.

Once integrated, both Italy and Germany realized that they were trailing the United Kingdom and France in terms of economic power. They lacked colonies, so there were no foreign lands from which they could draw resources and raw materials or to which industrial products could be sold. This was considered a problem especially in fast-developing Germany. Although it is still a matter of debate among historians, Germany's desire for colonies seemed to play a crucial role in triggering World War I in 1914.

Germany's leaders believed that colonies could be gained with a war victory. When Austrian Archduke Franz Ferdinand died from an assassin's bullet in Sarajevo, Bosnia and Herzegovina, Germany and its ally the Habsburg Empire decided to start a war. The third ally, Italy, changed sides in 1915. It was promised the eastern coast of the Adriatic Sea if it joined the Western Allied forces. This move, of course, supported opinions about the war being fought primarily for the purpose of gaining territorial possessions. Four years and millions of lives later, Germany and its allies capitulated and were occupied by foreign forces or, as in the case of the Habsburg Empire, broken into several new countries.

Only two decades later, imperialistic tendencies of another German political regime, the Nazis, caused World War II (1939–1945), this time taking Italians and other satellites with them. Nazism and its Italian equivalent, fascism, grew out of widespread economic misery that followed World War I. Nazis and fascists were able to gain strong political ground, which eventually led to dictatorships and imperialistic aspirations. The ideologies also promoted strong government control of the economy, and Nazism fostered bitter discrimination based on race, ethnicity, and religion, especially toward Jews. The dictatorships that rose in Germany and Italy were in sharp contrast to the democratic past both countries had enjoyed since the nineteenth century.

After the end of World War II in 1945, the political picture of Europe drastically changed. It became polarized between Communist Eastern Europe and democratic Western Europe. Fascism, which had gained power in Portugal and Spain in the 1920s and 1930s, survived on the European continent until 1970, when these countries became democratic. Countries that bordered the Soviet Union, from Poland to Bulgaria, were incorporated into the Soviet bloc after the Moscow-led local Communists took over. In 1955, they created the Warsaw Pact. This defensive organization was developed to counter the North Atlantic Treaty Organization (NATO), created in 1949 for the purpose of defending Western Europe. Communism was a one-party system in which the state had control over the economy and worked closely with the working class. Free enterprise and a market system were prohibited, a limitation with which the West disagreed. In the Soviet bloc, instead of a free and open market, countries had a so-called compensation system. Exchange was not financial;

German tank units enter a village as part of the Nazi lightning invasion, or blitzkrieg, of Poland, which began on September 1, 1939. The Nazi belief system was rooted strongly in racial, ethnic, and religious discrimination.

rather, it featured goods traded for goods, such as tractors for wheat or furniture for medicine. This system did not make too many members happy.

A rarely acknowledged reason for the strong division in Europe was the Soviet Union's xenophobia (fear of foreigners). Russians, whose country has been invaded and occupied many times in the past, are highly suspicious of strangers. To prevent being invaded again, the Soviet Union wanted a buffer zone—an "iron curtain"—in the form of neighboring countries. To preserve such conditions, it had to establish Communist-led governments in Poland, Czechoslovakia, Hungary, Romania, and Bulgaria and had to control them militarily. East Germany, although essentially an artificial creation, was a welcome addition. Divided Europe lasted until the late 1980s, when political winds changed and these countries finally won the right to decide their own future. Their goal rapidly became membership in the growing European Union.

THE EUROPEAN UNION

What ultimately could become the United States of Europe began humbly in 1951 as the European Coal and Steel Community. This was an economic organization of six countries: France, Germany, Italy, the Netherlands, Belgium, and Luxembourg. From the very beginning, the intent was to integrate economic forces into what eventually became an organization that could lead Europe toward political integration. After World War II brought destruction on a massive scale, it became clear in the minds of politicians that Western Europe needed fast recovery and development. In 1957, the organization changed its name to the European Economic Community (EEC).This name lasted until 1993, when the organization finally became known as the European Union (EU).

During its first two decades, the organization expanded slowly and faced many problems, some of which remain. It is difficult to develop an organization that can unite people in a culture region known for a history of separatism, nationalistic aspiration, and repeated conflicts. Creating the United States of America was not difficult because the new country lacked a history of conflict between its constituent elements. It was not replacing any particular historical context. In Europe, however, countries often look suspiciously on any form of political integration out of fear of losing sovereignty. Expansion of the EEC was helped by the fact that Europe was already ideologically divided between "us" (the West) and "them" (the Communists). The need for cooperation was clear, as countries recognized the

This is an overhead view showing the scene in the ancient city hall of Rome, Italy, on March 25, 1957, as the Treaty of Rome for the European Economic Community (EEC) was signed by delegates of six West European nations—France, Germany, Italy, Belgium, the Netherlands, and Luxembourg.

wisdom of "strength in numbers." In terms of mutual defense, NATO was a strong and highly cooperative beginning.

In 1973, the United Kingdom, Denmark, and Ireland joined the EEC; they were followed in 1981 by Greece and in 1986 by Spain and Portugal. Finally, in 1995, two years after the organization changed its name to the European Union, Austria, Sweden, and Finland became members. These three countries, together with Norway and Iceland, were members of another, smaller, economic organization called the European Free Trade Association (EFTA). Among all economic and political achievements, one stands out as quite remarkable: For a region with a long history of bitter conflicts, it is amazing that borders between countries are now open, allowing the free flow of people and goods. The greatest challenge to the open borders came in 2004, when the EU accepted ten new members, nearly all of which were former Communist countries of Eastern Europe.

In early 2005, few effects of the European Union's eastward expansion were noticeable. Still, many Western Europeans are concerned about the possible "invasion" from poorer Eastern Europe. Culture plays an important role in political decisions, as Turkey well knows. This country has been a member of NATO since 1950 and applied for membership in the EU in 1987. It still awaits an answer, which may take many more years to come. The main argument for rejecting Turkey is not political; rather, it is Europe's reluctance to accept 72 million additional Muslims. Significant numbers of Europeans unfortunately share the opinion that only barbarians come from the East!

As an economic bloc, the European Union is growing rapidly. More will be said about the EU economy in the next chapter. In 1999, it introduced the common currency, the euro, which a majority of countries accepted. Some, such as the United Kingdom, could reject it because EU member countries have the final word when it comes to their own destiny. The next step is the establishment of single citizenship. This would allow people from any country to have the rights of all. This is one of the more difficult programs to realize. National feelings are difficult to replace, and few people are willing to lose the sense of belonging to their nation-state.

THE STATES

The structure of European states varies from republics to kingdoms. Today, democratic principles of parliamentary democracy are nearly universal, regardless of who rules the country. Times of autocratic regimes are past, and former Communist countries now are democratic republics. After years of socialism in Eastern Europe, it is understandable that the era of kings is long past. Kings have not ruled in the region for several generations, since before World War II, and there is no desire whatsoever for their return. In Western Europe, several countries are still kingdoms. Kings and queens, like those in the United Kingdom, enjoy mainly ceremonial power. Executive powers are in the hands of the elected government.

Democracy and the electoral process work slightly differently in Europe than in the United States, yet the results are similar. The most important difference is reciprocity among political parties; that is, it is not winner-takes-all rule. When Americans vote for congresspersons, only the winners go to the state capital or Washington, D.C. The losers can be one vote or one million votes behind the winner, and the result is the same. In Europe, parties nominate candidates, who, based on the percentage of votes that their party wins, are delegated to the legislature. If the winning party receives 45 percent of the votes and the runner up receives 25 percent, these parties will be represented in the assembly by 45 percent and 25 percent of its members, respectively. Such a system is designed to provide pluralism and to press parties to form coalition governments, thereby creating dialogs and cooperation. Parties need to pass only the usual 5 percent threshold to participate in assembly. This system often creates parliaments with membership from all over the political spectrum. Most, if not all, voices are represented, and people are encouraged to vote for smaller parties that may better represent their views. The governments, the prime minister, and the prime minister's cabinet are accountable to the parliament.

The parliament can cast a vote of no confidence if it is not satisfied with the cabinet's work. When this is done, it can lead to new elections, which are not held on a rigidly predetermined schedule as in the United States. In some countries, government changes often. In Italy, since the end of World War II, the government has changed on an average of once each year! In Europe, as in the United States, a change in government rarely leads to political turmoil; as often as not, it leads to improvement.

GEOGRAPHY OF CONFLICT

On casual glance, the European culture region appears to be calm. In the European Union, however, conflict exists in various forms (it is, after all, an organization of 25 independent states). Conflicts range from "gentlemanly disagreements" to deeply rooted antagonism that can lead to armed confrontation.

Separatism, often backed by terrorism, is the greatest source of conflict in the region. Although Europe is slowly approaching regional unification, separatist feelings exist in many areas. Northern Ireland is perhaps the best-known example. This part of the United Kingdom of Great Britain and Northern Ireland (the UK's full name) has experienced turbulence for many decades. On one side are Irish separatist organizations, such as the Irish Republican Army (IRA) that are trying to oust the British. They would like to join the Republic of Ireland, thereby uniting the island as a single political unit. This movement is backed by local Catholics who have close ties to the dominantly Catholic Republic of Ireland. The British government, on the other hand, works to stop the movement. It is backed by Northern Ireland's Protestant population, who could lose too much if the unification were to occur. This long-standing conflict has often led to bloody acts of terrorism, all in the heart of Western democracy.

In Spain, the Basques are fighting for independence. They want the Basque homeland, which occupies small portions of both Spain and France, to become an independent Basque state. Separatism has proven to be a bloody affair in this situation. The Basque terrorist organization Euzkadi Ta Askatasuna (ETA) is believed to be responsible for killing more than 1,000 people. ETA often targets officials appointed by the national or local government who disagree with Basque objectives.

Protestant civil rights marchers pass under a peace statue as they leave London-derry, Northern Ireland, in support of the Drumcree standoff and for Protestant civil and religious liberty.

The Mediterranean island of Corsica is politically, but not ethnically, French. A long-standing independence movement there has often led to violence.

What is perhaps the most difficult conflict to resolve is that found within the territory of the former Yugoslavia. Conflicts were ignited when the country dissolved in the early 1990s, and all of its former political subunits became engaged in some form of armed struggle. Some were of short duration, as in Slovenia, whereas others were long and bloody, such as in Croatia and Bosnia. Macedonia and Serbia and Montenegro are still working on how to politically resolve ethnic conflicts. In the late 1990s, conflict between Slavic and ethnic Albanian populations broke out. This struggle eventually required NATO's military intervention against Yugoslavia (now Serbia and Montenegro) in 1999. Although calm appears to have finally settled on the region, conflict continues to smolder just beneath the surface. Ethnic Albanians, for example, want to secede (politically withdraw) from the areas where they now live and unite with Albania.

Some separatist conflicts in Europe are strongly felt but are not violent. In Belgium, for example, a popular joke says that, in Belgium, everything is double. The country is divided between the French-speaking Walloons and the Dutch Flemish. Within the small country (about the size of Maryland), people not only speak two languages but also are sharply divided between Catholicism and Protestantism and are ethnically divided between "French" and "German/Dutch" lifestyles. Divisions are visible in parts of northern Italy, which was a part of Austria until 1918. There are areas within the Alps where people speak German, have German last names, and openly talk about their aspiration for South Tirol to become part of Austria. In Romania, 2 million ethnic Hungarians would rather live in the neighboring country that bears their name.

Political conflicts can also be economic in nature. As a result of geopolitical changes, the tiny new country of Slovenia was left with limited access to international seas. Slovenian access to the Adriatic was left to the discretion of Croatia. Slovenians, therefore, decided to "modify" their border with Croatia. They announced that the border "technically" is located a few thousand yards south, thereby allowing them access to the sea. The Croatians then decided to create an exclusive economic zone in their part of the Adriatic Sea, which completely isolated Slovenians. The real reason behind these political tricks is the competition between the Croatian port of Rijeka and the Slovenian port of Koper for dominance over trade among several landlocked Central European countries and the world.

PROJECTION OF MILITARY POWER

Europeans tend to count on diplomacy to solve global political issues. At the same time, they recognize the wisdom of Theodore Roosevelt's famous statement that one should "speak softly and carry a big stick." Sometimes, they realize, military intervention is necessary in order to prevent or stop conflict elsewhere. Individually, however, no European country has the military strength to act on its own as a major power. Even the United Kingdom, which has a long history of global military domination, finds itself rather limited in terms of committing large contingents of military personnel and equipment overseas. Military inadequacy is even more evident in most other countries because of budget cuts and publicly expressed pacifism.

Many observers expect that, in time, the European Union will become a strong, unified military power. Others, however, believe that it will take a considerable length of time before the EU will be able to present a cohesive foreign policy. Within the region, there are simply too many individual "agendas" and divergent interests. In addition, all member countries retain the individual right to veto foreign policy decisions with which they disagree; therefore, it may be all but impossible to reach a consensus on vital issues. This is well illustrated by the U.S. military intervention in Iraq. Some countries were strongly supportive of the U.S. involvement, whereas others were adamantly opposed.

CHAPTER 7

Economic Geography

The distribution of wealth and economic well-being in Europe is fairly uneven and will continue to be until Eastern Europe catches up with Western Europe. When this may happen is anyone's guess. Some believe that it will occur within one or two decades; others doubt that it will ever happen. There is little assurance that political integration will produce satisfactory economic results. Some historical examples may provide a clue to the future.

Portugal lagged far behind the rest of Western Europe economically until it entered the EU in 1986. A fascist dictatorship had controlled the country since the 1920s. Its GDP increased 25 percent during the first 15 years of membership. The economy was stagnant, the infrastructure resembled that of third world countries, and women were treated as second-class citizens. With EU membership, Portugal became a democracy and the economy was liberalized. Society changed rapidly because people realized that there were few benefits in remaining relatively backward and traditional. The economy continued to emphasize agriculture, but production increased greatly. Economic success allowed Portugal to qualify for membership in a single-currency euro zone. The country still ranks in the bottom half of EU members in terms of GDP and scale of living, but its remarkable growth in such a short period of time can serve as an example of what may occur in the future with Eastern European countries.

ECONOMIC IMBALANCE

The speed of economic change in former East European Communist countries is the main concern in regard to a single European market. The GDP of those countries ranks far below those of Western Europe, less than half in many instances. Germany, the United Kingdom, France, and Italy are among the ten most economically developed countries in the world, and many other EU members are not far behind. Eastern European economies in general are not closing the gap as rapidly as many had hoped they would. In fact, many observers now believe that the economic chasm may exist much longer than expected and may widen in some instances.

Some countries are showing signs of progress. Slovenia, a tiny country of 2 million citizens tucked between the Alps and the Adriatic Sea, was once the best-developed republic of former Yugoslavia. After winning independence, it underwent productive economic reforms that concentrated on the growth of services. During the 1990s, its GDP rose to about 75 percent of the European Union's average. Unfortunately, Slovenia is a small country whose success is more an exception than a rule as an indicator of the future.

Two major issues stand between prosperity and Eastern Europe. First is the need to develop tertiary (service-related) industries and lessen dependence on agriculture and manufacturing. Second, there must be a better distribution of wealth. During Communist rule, the state owned almost all means of production. As soon as Communism was gone, privatization took place. Factories and businesses became privately owned but were in the hands of a small number of skilled businessmen. The majority of the population did not share in this accumulation of wealth. This process brought about further erosion of the middle class that already had suffered decline during the economic downturn after the fall of Communism.

To make matters worse, many of the formerly state-owned factories were barely profitable and had more employees than necessary. In order to make a profit, owners began to lay off large numbers of excess (and often inefficient) workers, thereby creating additional pressure on the welfare state. Now, economies long dependent on primary industries (agriculture and resource use) and secondary industries (manufacturing) are in desperate need of improvement. There also is a drastic need to develop tertiary industries—services such as education, medicine, business, transportation, and related activities. In the United States, only 2 percent of the population is involved in agriculture-related activities, whereas in Romania that number is closer to 40 percent. Economic progress depends on a country making the switch from primary to tertiary and other advanced postindustrial economic activities. Switzerland, a country known for its banking, is perhaps the best example. Largely lacking natural resources and without an exit to the world's seas, Switzerland managed to create one of the world's strongest economies and wealthiest societies. In developed countries, primary industries account for a very small part of the national economic output.

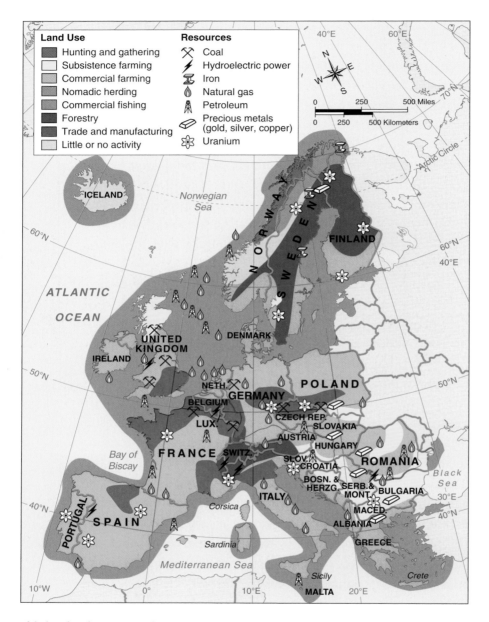

This is a land use map of Europe. Commercial farming plays an important role in the lives of many Europeans.

These workers harvest hay in Sugatag, Romania. Nearly 40 percent of Romania's population is involved in agricultural activities, as compared with the United States, which has only 2 percent.

MAJOR ECONOMIC ZONES

The Industrial Revolution of the 1800s, which began in the United Kingdom, triggered economic trends that forever changed the European urban landscape. A key player was James Watt, who made improvements to the steam engine. The more efficient steam engine vastly increased the efficiency of textile manufacturing. Soon, coal and steel manufacturing spread throughout the country. Areas centered on sprawling industrial cities became recognized for particular activities. Interior cities such as Birmingham and Sheffield were known for steel production, and Manchester became a major textile center. Other cities were known for mining of coal, iron ore, and other raw materials needed for the growing economy. In the nineteenth century, the United Kingdom was the world's leading economic power because of the Industrial Revolution. The interior was the producer, and London, Liverpool, and other ports and banking centers served as doors to the world. Today, London is one of the world's leading financial centers. The city also has led the country into the postindustrial age, in which service plays a much more important role than do primary and secondary industries.

The Industrial Revolution serves as a perfect example of how cultural diffusion works. Steam power and many other new ideas that made industries more efficient and productive soon spread from the British Isles to the European continent. In the decades that followed, much of neighboring Northwestern Europe began to develop rapidly. Other parts of the region began to fall behind as they clung to traditional economic activities. Industrialization spread first to France and Belgium and from there to Germany, where the largest and most advanced industrial zone was developed. Northwest Germany's Ruhr River valley, in the province of North Rhine–Westphalia, became a huge network of large industrial cities. In this area, about the size of Rhode Island, 10 million people are employed in industry, sales, services, and information activities. To fulfill the need for labor in the 1960s and 1970s, Germany invited many foreigners to settle and work in industrial towns. Today, the Ruhr Valley is home to hundreds of thousands of immigrants and their descendants, many of whom were born in Germany and consider themselves German.

Coal and steel transformed the sleepy Ruhr countryside into a gigantic production area. It is linked to the world by the navigable Rhine River, which flows through the heart of the region to the world's leading port city, Rotterdam (in the Netherlands), and the Atlantic Ocean. Geographic location and transportation ability have helped Germany become a leading EU economic partner with virtually all other European countries. As is true in England, Germany's financial center is not

The Industrial Revolution began in 19th century England and gradually spread throughout most of Europe and much of the world. Germany's Ruhr region, pictured here, became one of the world's chief industrial areas.

located in the traditional heartland of heavy industry. Frankfurt am Main (Frankfurt am der Oder also exists), the center of the country's stock exchange and banking industry, is located on the Main River in the province of Hessen, well to the south of the industrial belt.

Traditional German industries, identified by dingy buildings with high chimneys that belch coal smoke, are disappearing rapidly. They are being replaced by modern, gleaming structures that house highly profitable manufacturing companies and businesses that generate revenue through service and technology. They often can be found far removed from the sprawling, congested cities in Bavaria or in other pleasant rural areas. These are new kinds of industries, a prominent feature of the postindustrial economy and resulting society.

Perhaps no other region has benefited more from the adoption of industrialization than northern Italy. In the Po River valley, a number of cities including Milan (Milano) have become economic centers. Most European countries have a leading economic area or center. Depending on the particular country's size and economic strength, such areas vary in size and strength. In the case of northern Italy, the area is large and strong. Of crucial importance in terms of the future, it also produces a very small amount of black smoke. This means that the region has successfully made the transition from a secondary, or manufacturing, economy to a tertiary, or service, economy.

Secondary industries in large cities remain a vital part of the economy in northern Italy. Today, most growth is seen among various mid-sized businesses scattered through the countryside and in small towns. Italians now realize that small and mid-sized businesses are the key to prosperity because they benefit the middle class, especially if they are well diversified. Fashion, industrial design, food production, and furniture or appliance manufacturing are some of the success stories. The final products (except food) generally are manufactured elsewhere, usually in Asia. Italians manage the business aspects of the industry and realize a profit of billions of dollars. Many business owners never see their products. Goods may be shipped from the point of production (such as Taiwan) to the point of sale (Canada), and most of the profits end up in Italy.

Most Europeans recognize that a person need not live in a large city to become economically successful. Because of improved transportation and an excellent electronic information network, the countryside also affords many opportunities and amenities. During his travels through Europe, the author has visited many businesses located far from major cities. They ranged from magazine publishing and printing services in Italy to furniture makers in Slovenia and a musical instrument shop in Germany. Each of these businesses was in a rural area and highly profitable.

An improved infrastructure will, in theory, assist Eastern Europe in catching up with Western Europe. Eastern Europe needs huge financial investments to jump-start the regional economy, as well. There simply is too much catching up to do without outside help. One of the major disadvantages is the lack of expressways in Eastern Europe. As the United States, England, Germany, and several other countries recognized long ago, without easy access, location means little. Fortunately, Western Europe recognizes that it is in its best interest to help Eastern Europe develop. This is why even Bosnia and Herzegovina will eventually benefit from expressways that will link the Adriatic Sea and Central Europe. When completed between 2010 and 2020, the country and its resources will be able to play a more important role in the regional economy. Bosnia and Herzegovina potentially has much to offer economically, including a well-educated labor force with wages much lower than those in Western Europe.

ENERGY

Europeans are a leading force in the growing demand for a cleaner, safer environment. Most European countries have ratified the Kyoto Protocol, which means that they have agreed to lower the emission of carbon dioxide and other gases to pre-1990 levels. Throughout the region, public demand for the use of cleaner energy is increasing as well. Considering the past dependence on coal as the primary energy source, such demands are understandable. Use of coal resulted in massive pollution, including acid rain.

Despite the environmental issues, the demand for energy—particularly that provided by fossil fuels—is rising rapidly. The solution to this dilemma rests in the creation of alternative energy sources, but this can be very expensive. Many alternatives, such as wind, solar, geothermal, and hydroelectric power, are costly to develop and have environmental restrictions. It takes a great deal of time and expense to transition from fossil fuels to one of these other sources. Some progress is being made, however: Wind farms (electricity-producing wind towers) now dot the European landscape, high gasoline prices discourage gas-guzzling vehicles, and many homes are built to use energy more efficiently.

As dependence on coal has steadily declined, consumption of petroleum and natural gas has increased drastically. Unfortunately, except for relatively small production in the North Sea and Romania, Europe must import its energy. The Middle East, North Africa, and Russia are the main suppliers. Natural gas is affordable and clean, but it is imported from Russia and Central Asia (Central Asian pipelines go through Russia) and the Russians dictate the price. One of the EU's demands before allowing Russia to enter the World Trade Organization (WTO) was stabilization of the price of natural gas.

Since several well-publicized nuclear accidents, including Three Mile Island, in Pennsylvania in 1979, and Chernobyl, in Ukraine in 1986, the building of nuclear plants has stopped, at least in Western Europe. Public opinion tends to be against further development of nuclear-powered electrical plants, and it would be difficult to find a community that would volunteer to have a nuclear plant built nearby. Still, Europeans are divided on this issue. Many people support atomic energy development. They point to the fact that, under ideal conditions, it harms the environment much less than more traditional forms of energy do and it has a high output. Others fear a repeat of what happened in Chernobyl, where thousands died or had to be evacuated. Especially in energy-hungry Eastern Europe, many people support the development of nuclear energy. They want to ensure, however, that the facilities are safe and well maintained. A major factor that influences opinions is the degree to which a country depends on nuclear energy. France, for example, generates more than 70 percent of electricity through atomic means, whereas the Italians have closed all of their plants. Half of Sweden's electricity is of nuclear origin, but Norway has none.

Although critics voice concerns about nuclear energy because of its potential hazards, many European countries still rely heavily on nuclear fuels to generate inexpensive electrical power.

Some countries are blessed with other sources of energy, such as hydroelectricity. One thing is certain: If Europe is going to continue to progress economically, it will require a reliable source of relatively inexpensive energy—and the world is running rather short on alternatives.

TRADE

The removal of borders in the European Union has highly benefited national economies. It also has helped individual citizens who can take advantage of the open borders and free intraregional trade. The movement, sale, and purchase of goods, as well as tax-paying processes, have been greatly simplified. Most countries in the region have a majority of their trade with each other. Eastern Europe imports much more from Western

Europe than it exports, and it exports primarily raw materials and agricultural products—commodities of relatively low value. It must import expensive electronics, automobiles, and other manufactured goods. This trade sends a disproportionate amount of money from Eastern Europe to Western Europe, which creates a negative trade balance.

Former colonial powers trade with their ex-colonies in terms similar to the above-mentioned. Most of the former colonies keep close political and economic ties and hope to gain certain benefits. As less-developed countries, the ex-colonies have less to offer other than natural resources, raw materials, or low-value manufactured goods. The European Union is attempting to revitalize African and Asian economies by implementing a number of economic programs.

Other major trade partners are oil-producing countries such as the Organization of Petroleum Exporting Countries (OPEC) members and Russia. Trade between the United States and Europe is huge in both the range of goods and the resulting revenue exchange. Europe and the United States exchange items from needles to locomotives and wines to jet aircraft. Just through the joint NATO defense system, Americans supply Europeans with arms worth billions of dollars. Europeans export luxury goods desirable in the United States. These two economic giants often become involved in trade wars to protect their markets and to force the other side to lower tariffs. During recent years, these economic conflicts have involved everything from bananas to steel and European perfumes.

Europe long has been and will certainly continue to be an economic powerhouse. Most of its people are prosperous and enjoy a scale of living that rivals that of other developed regions of the world. With regional economic unification becoming a reality under the European Union, the region's economic fortunes should continue to thrive.

CHAPTER 8

Regional Geography

It would be a difficult task to find a culture region that was homogeneous in all aspects. Variations, some large and others small, always exist from place to place. The general way of life is similar throughout most of the European culture region, but there are differences. As you already have learned, language, religion, economic activities, diet, and political ideologies vary considerably within the region. In order to spotlight such differences within a cultural realm, geographers identify subregions. In the United States, for example, people often refer to subregions such as the South, New England, or the Midwest. Although these regions are distinctly American, each has a unique cultural "flavor."

An obvious regional difference is the one that exists between Eastern Europe and Western Europe. Eastern Europe is composed of former Communist countries, lands that former British Prime Minister Sir Winston Churchill described as being behind an "iron curtain." The countries to which Churchill was referring were neither free nor democratic. Today, Eastern European countries are free, but a divide persists in economic terms. Elsewhere on the continent, many people see a Northern-Southern division based on economic, religious, dietary, and other cultural differences.

Regional divisions also exist within individual countries. Italy, for example, is unofficially divided into the prosperous and progressive north and a much poorer and more traditional south. In nearly all aspects other than the economic, residents of the north and south are very similar, yet this division between the two regions is widely held.

Many regional divisions that exist within countries are related to differences between urban and rural areas, whereas others may include physical conditions such as isolated highlands as opposed to more accessible and productive coastal lowlands. All regions are arbitrarily defined, and the divisions used in this book are no different. They are regions that many geographers, including the author, who is European by birth, have identified. In so doing, it is possible to divide a large and complex region into smaller "chunks" so that regional differences can be better understood.

SOUTHERN EUROPE

Southern Europe is the broad belt of countries that generally border the Mediterranean Sea. It includes all countries from Atlantic-facing Portugal in the west to the Aegean shores of Greece and Turkey in the east. In many respects, these countries share similar series of historical events, many of which have created cultural landscapes that are unique to this realm. With few exceptions, Southern Europe has always had an economy dependent on agriculture- and fishing-related activities. This has influenced many customs, traditions, and dietary habits. Because of rugged environmental conditions, the region has little land on which large-scale farming could develop. As a result, agriculture has emphasized high-value specialty crops that are well suited to the Mediterranean climate: fruits, especially grapes; olives; vegetables; and so forth.

Until recent times, most people in Mediterranean Europe lived in coastal areas. Many communities, in fact, trace their origin back to the era of the Roman Empire or even earlier. Southern Europe has long been considered "backward" by many Northern Europeans. This perception has begun to change because of tourism. In both summer and winter, millions of Europeans flock to the Mediterranean coasts of Spain and France. Other popular destinations are coastal Italy, the Greek islands, and Croatia's Dalmatian Coast.

Mediterranean culture has certain unique characteristics. The most significant are the roles of family and religion and the easygoing lifestyle. Southern Europe is also a more patriarchal world, in which males hold a dominant role in the family and community. Traditions, particularly in rural areas, are important to people who are accustomed to a certain way of life. Customs that may appear strange to an outsider visiting an Italian or Greek village are "just the way it should be" to locals.

Architectural styles in the Mediterranean region differ from those in the rest of Europe. In the absence of extensive forests, most traditional structures are built of stone. This durable material is abundant, and a well-constructed building can last indefinitely. Many structures date to Roman times. Villages have an "old" look, which adds to the region's charm.

The place of sport and leisure in the lives of ordinary people is rather important. Southern Europeans are obsessed with soccer. When an international competition is scheduled, many people take vacation time in order to watch their national team play. Soccer is tremendously popular throughout much of the

This is a Greek village along the Mediterranean Sea. Mediterranean architecture is characterized by building mostly with stone, giving homes and shops an older look.

world, but nowhere does it play a more significant role in daily life than here. It is said that, if any Mediterranean country was invaded during a televised soccer match, the war would end in a matter of minutes. No one would leave the TV set to defend the homeland.

Family ties between parents and children are strong, and they often live in one household, even if children are married. It is not unusual for three generations of a family to share a house or to live next door to each other. Elderly parents are cared for by their children. Unlike in the United States, nursing homes are considered a last resort rather than a necessity. One reason the family is so strong is Roman Catholicism. This faith encourages such ties. A majority of countries in Southern Europe, particularly Italy, Spain, and Portugal, are still bastions of Catholicism.

The physical appearance of Southerners also differs somewhat from that of other Europeans. Most people have dark hair and eyes and skin with visible olive tones. Naturally blond people with light skin color are in the minority.

NORTHERN EUROPE

Northern Europe is a region defined by both its culture and history. It includes all European countries other than those of the Mediterranean realm and former Communist Eastern Europe. One criterion that separates Northern Europe from the Mediterranean realm is the division between Protestant and Catholic Europe. Protestantism is dominant in Germany, Scandinavia, and the United Kingdom. Another major difference is language, with most North European countries speaking a Germanic-based, rather than a Romanic- or Slavic-based, tongue. Historically, the Alps served as both a physical and a cultural barrier. The Germanic cultural sphere prevailed north of the mountains, and the Romanic influence dominated south of that range.

Northern Europe gave birth to two very important cultural developments: the Industrial Revolution and liberal democracy. Combined, they made possible the very rapid economic development and urbanization experienced throughout the region during the nineteenth and twentieth centuries. This subregion is the most economically advanced in Europe, and its citizens enjoy the continent's highest standards of living. This has been achieved despite a long history of political confrontations and instability that led to two world wars. Fortunately, such conflicts appear to be a thing of the past.

In Northern Europe, people not only enjoy the benefits of postindustrialized society, but also share their wealth with others. Scandinavian countries in particular are known for their social liberalism. This may stem in part from the Lutheran tradition of engaging in social service. This trait is noticeable even in the areas of the United States where Americans of Scandinavian ancestry are dominant. Minnesota has a high proportion of residents of Swedish and Norwegian descent, and that state is known for its liberalism and wide range of social programs.

Despite its having given birth to the Protestant Reformation, this part of Europe is becoming increasingly secular. Religion plays a very minor role, if any, in the lives of most citizens. More and more people declare themselves atheists or agnostics. In some countries, less than 10 percent of the population attends church or claims affiliation with some faith.

In terms of population, the most densely settled area is within a triangle formed by London, Paris, and Berlin. These cities themselves are among the largest in Europe. Eight of every ten Northern Europeans lives in a city. Population patterns are a reflection of the rapid urbanization that followed the Industrial Revolution. The landscape in Northern Europe offers a marvelous contrast of medieval city centers and modern urban architecture. Much of the countryside retains an idyllic atmosphere that seems little changed from the times of Hans Christian Andersen or the Grimm brothers.

To Southern Europeans, Northerners appear to be cold, reserved, and unemotional. Northern Europeans, especially the Germans, however, are well known for their work ethic. Education is emphasized throughout this subregion. Northern Europe is known for having quality educational systems and high rates of literacy, and many people speak two or more languages. In Switzerland, it is not at all unusual for people to be fluent in German, French, Italian, and English. Physically, North Europeans tend to be lighter in hair, eye, and skin color than those who live in the Mediterranean region.

EAST-CENTRAL EUROPE

For half a century, during the period of Communist domination, this subregion was called "Eastern Europe." The term, used in the

West, was applied to all so-called Soviet bloc countries that lay behind the "Iron Curtain." With the end of Communism, several new countries (lands once a part of the Soviet Union), have emerged. The result of this political change is that "Eastern Europe" has now expanded eastward to include countries such as Ukraine, Belarus, and Russia. Today, therefore, it is more appropriate to refer to countries such as Poland, Czech Republic, Slovakia, and Hungary as being in East-Central Europe. In Europe, it seems that no one wants to be included in any group designated with the prefix "east." Culturally and historically, these East-Central European countries are correct in this preference. Throughout much of their history, their ties to Western Europe have been much stronger than those to the Russian sphere.

Cities such as Prague (Czech Republic), Warsaw (Poland), and Budapest (Hungary) amply display evidence of the region's rich history. Prague, once the main city of the Holy Roman Empire, is one of Europe's leading tourist destinations. Every year, millions of tourists from all over the world visit the city to enjoy its architectural and artistic beauty and rich Slavic, German, and Jewish history. Since the early 1990s, Prague has experienced a renaissance and is becoming especially popular with young people. According to unofficial data, as many as 100,000 young Americans now live in the city. Some are there to study and others simply to experience the European way of life.

The most interesting change in this region is that of the people. Except in the former Yugoslavia, where personal freedoms were not limited, contact with the "Western" world was nearly nonexistent. During the era of Soviet domination, there was very little cultural exchange between Eastern Europe and Western Europe. Once the barriers fell and the borders opened, it became almost essential for Eastern Europeans to experience the glamour of the Western European lifestyle. Expensive Western European luxury vehicles immediately began to replace the flimsy Yugos and Trabants of the Soviet era. Fancy boutiques and restaurants are booming. In urban areas, the only reminder of the past is in the

The Charles Bridge, built in the fourteenth century, crosses the Vltava River.
Located in Prague, Czech Republic, it is among the many tourist attractions in one
of Europe's leading tourist destinations.

so-called architecture of social realism, that is, unattractive, gray living quarters for the working class built in the 1960s and 1970s.

Much of the countryside offers a sharp contrast to city life. As is true in many rural environments, life is lived at a much slower pace and change comes slowly. Perhaps the most noticeable difference between living standards among European countries is the well being of rural people. Villagers throughout the East-Central subregion still struggle to make the transition from what they were used to for so long. Governments know that the majority of voters live in urban areas; therefore, politicians shower their attention and resources on cities, leaving the countryside neglected.

In Romania, Bulgaria, and some former Yugoslav republics, life is even more difficult. In these countries, economies are poor and poverty is widespread. Interestingly enough, however, rural folk always seem to show hospitality no matter how impoverished they may be. Nowhere in Europe are foreigners more welcome than in the southeast. One can only wonder about how these people can be so warm and have been involved in so many bitter ethnic conflicts. This is especially true considering the fact that it can be difficult to notice the significant physical or cultural (except religious) differences among them. With the increase in standard of living, people will, perhaps, eventually forget past antagonism and concentrate on future prosperity. Affluence is every culture's best medicine.

CHAPTER 9

Geography of the Future

Europe is an extremely complex cultural region, and Europeans face many issues in the near future. Perhaps the greatest challenge, and the greatest opportunity, is continued unification of the continent. This is the first time in history that it is being attempted peacefully. Rather than military force, the dream of greater economic prosperity drives Europeans toward the goal of a united continent. At this stage, it is difficult to predict the ultimate results of this ongoing effort. A desire for peaceful cooperation should eventually prevail, erasing long-lasting breaks that have often led to open conflict.

HOW WILL EUROPE LOOK IN THE FUTURE?

In geopolitical terms, the next few decades will bring major changes. Political boundaries between countries may eventually disappear. Were this to happen, it would be to the benefit of many ethnic minorities whose territorial aspirations often have led to ethnic conflict. If all Europeans finally are able to put aside their ethnic differences and develop a sense of "belonging" and loyalty to the greater whole, nationalistic aspirations will diminish. Today, these aspirations are strong simply because so many people feel unsure about the future. If unification worked in the United States—a country created by former Europeans who represented many ethnicities—it should certainly work in Europe.

One problem that must be addressed is that of the current process of "selectivity" in regard to who is or is not "European." Germans or Swedes are no more "European" than Turks. Before any change can be completely successful, a generation of young people must be raised with this sense of belonging to a unified community. Europe has gone a long way in successfully erasing its historical rifts, but millions of people still remember the sharp divisions of the past, including two world wars that ravaged the continent. The British are hesitant to open their door to total integration; they have not adopted the euro, for example. Many countries fear the potential dominance of Germany and France and are hesitant to give up their independent "voice." In Europe, the burden of the past has always been heavy.

POPULATION ISSUES

In terms of population geography, if current demographic trends continue, they will present some serious problems for the region. By 2000, Europe had become the first continent in modern history to experience zero population growth (ZPG). A significant number of European countries are actually losing population. As the region continues the transition from an industrial to a postindustrial society, the trend toward small families should continue. In many countries, a drastically shrinking population may pose huge problems. The lack of an adequate labor force ultimately could serve as a major roadblock to further economic progress. To prevent this from happening, some countries are already implementing population programs that encourage families to have more children. In general, such programs have not been successful. Postindustrialism contributes to increased affluence, but rising affluence is an obstacle to population growth. The problems associated with population decline, and thus with workforce decline, can be countered only by increasing immigration quotas. In terms of issues that affect the region's future, immigration ranks high on the list of concerns shared by many.

The United States has benefited from immigration more than any other country in the world. Even though minor opposition toward immigration exists, Americans generally welcome immigrants (most Americans are descendants of immigrants, after all). Europeans are much more hesitant to open their doors to outsiders. To an outsider, this hesitance to accept others may appear to be the result of racism. Although racism exists, its influence is minor. The real concern held by many Europeans is the future of their own ethnic "purity." They worry about whether a wave of immigration—particularly from Asia and Africa—will forever swamp their own way of life. Will the French or British ethnicity, for example, become changed forever, or perhaps even lost, in time? Because of this concern, many European countries have very low immigration quotas. In a culture region that praises itself for its liberal social views, this seems rather paradoxical. The issues that surround immigration are difficult and complex. How this will all play out in the future is difficult to predict. Hopefully, the largest and most populated and economically successful countries will set a positive path for others to follow.

A GLOBAL ROLE

A unified Europe certainly would play an increasingly significant economic and political role on the global stage. After centuries of the countries going it alone, it will be interesting to see how joint foreign policy interests are going to be implemented. Until now, foreign policy issues have presented a major obstacle to European unity. This division is illustrated by the U.S. invasion of Iraq. The military action was strongly supported by some European countries and vehemently condemned by others. On both sides, there appears to be a need for more mature debate and recognition of Europe's growing position of responsibility in a turbulent world. Perhaps, this will come in the future. Many countries, after all, look on the new Europe as a symbol of freedom and democracy. Many political issues pose a challenge to the EU, not the least of which are its role in the Middle East and its relations with the former Soviet Union, much of Africa, and certainly the United States.

Political involvement in global issues is closely linked to economic involvement. A unified Europe will soon become the world's largest market, and its dependence on natural resources to fuel its economy will increase. Europe has imposed strict environmental regulations and has declining reserves of minerals and other resources. These factors will force Europeans to look elsewhere for the raw materials needed to fuel further economic growth. In the past, each country acted as its own agent to secure resources and raw materials. In the future, much of this will have to be a collective effort.

In terms of physical geography, a major concern is the impact of global warming in the future if, in fact, it is really happening. Significant numbers of Europeans believe that Earth's climate is warming and that the rise in temperatures is the result of human activity. Millions of Europeans live on low-lying plains. A rising sea level, which would result from melting glacial ice and warming of the water, would bring devastation to such areas. People would be displaced, agricultural land would be inundated, and

European Union (EU) leaders and heads of state stand for a group photograph at an EU summit in Brussels, Belgium, on December 17, 2004. The leaders then resumed their discussions regarding Turkey's application to join the EU.

the economic price would be awesome. Countries such as the Netherlands and Denmark would be first to pay the price. If climatic conditions change, existing agricultural patterns may be endangered. Flooding has always been a threat to much of the continent. If precipitation increases because of global warming, the area subject to flooding will increase.

Prevention of this and other potential environmental concerns is sought through world leadership in environmental protection. Many improvements have been implemented by Europeans since the dawn of the Industrial Revolution. A century ago, Europe was the dirtiest part of the globe. Dark clouds of smoke and smog that hovered above cities were considered a symbol of progress, but no longer. In regard to the global warming issue, Europe strongly supports implementation of the measures defined by the Kyoto Protocol. In doing so, they must reduce their reliance on fossil fuels. This, in turn, would cut back on the emission of "greenhouse" gases into the atmosphere. Many Europeans are willing to pay the price for this and other initiatives designed to protect the environment. As the modern world has learned, only an affluent society can afford the price of a clean environment. How costly environmental safeguards are going to be implemented by less wealthy lands, such as those in Eastern Europe, will be a problem in the future.

Another major issue that faces the region is Europe's reluctance to accept genetically modified food. Many people have concerns about the possible negative influence on humans. With recent severe outbreaks of livestock diseases such as mad cow and foot and mouth, these concerns are becoming even more pronounced. It will be interesting to see how the attitudes brewing in Europe will affect agriculture not only on the continent, but elsewhere as well. Many people see genetic engineering as the key to feeding and providing other raw materials for a growing world population. Others see it as a threat to the environment and human well-being.

Some Europeans see "Americanization" as a threat. This influence, of course, has been present ever since the first Hollywood motion picture reached European shores. Today, American influences are stronger than ever before. Traditionalists are afraid that their lifestyle, and Europe as a whole, will become nothing but an American-style giant discount store. It is difficult to convince many Europeans that, by spreading one's culture to others, one must understand that cultural interaction functions in both directions. American and other foreign influences will not lessen in the future; in fact, through the process of globalization, they will become even stronger.

Finally, at the end of this overview of the fascinating European culture region, you should be reminded of the first rule of geographic research. A book is only a companion to a geographer who seeks to learn more about places in a variety of ways. Ideally, distant places should be visited, but this is not always possible. In today's world, learning about other cultures should be a priority for us all. The world has never been more complex. At the same time, distant places have never been closer for personal observation through travel, media, or learning from others. By studying other cultures, we are better able to understand our own. Understanding Europe provides most Americans with a vital cultural link to our own past. It also may give us a glimpse of the global future.

second millennium B.C.	The first large wave of migrations across the European continent occurs.
first millennium B.C.	Ancient Greeks colonize much of the Mediterranean basin, and Rome gradually rises to become the world's leading power for many centuries.
A.D. 476	The Western Roman Empire collapses.
400s–600s	Major movement and resettlements of peoples from the eastern European lowlands into the rest of the continent occur; the nuclei of many modern nations form.
400s–1400s	Europe's Middle Ages occur.
1092	The Crusades, which continued for more than two centuries, begin.
1340s	An epidemic of bubonic plague devastates many areas, eventually killing approximately one-third of all Europeans.
1456	Johann Gutenberg invents movable type in Mainz, Germany; this revolutionizes the printing process and contributes to widespread increase in distribution of knowledge.
1500s	Drastic changes occur in the European religious landscape with the emergence of Protestantism.
1789	The French Revolution occurs.
Early 1800s	The Industrial Revolution begins in the United Kingdom; this gradually diffuses throughout northwestern Europe and contributes to rapid economic development.
1914–1918	World War I is fought.
1939–1945	World War II is fought.
1949	The U.S.-dominated North Atlantic Treaty Organization (NATO) is created.
1955	The Soviet Union-dominated Warsaw Pact is created.
1951	The European Coal and Steel Community is formed; it is renamed "European Economic Community" in 1957 and "European Union" in 1993.
1991–1995	Civil war in former Yugoslavia takes hundreds of thousands of lives, and millions more are displaced.
2004	European Union is enlarged with ten additional members and for the first time accepts former Communist countries of Eastern Europe.

Berentsen, William H., ed. *Contemporary Europe: A Geographic Analysis.* New York: John Wiley and Sons, 1997.

Cole, John, and Francis Cole. *A Geography of the European Union.* New York: Routledge, 1997.

Europa Publications. *The Europa World Yearbook.* London: Europa Publications, 1998.

Frankland, Gene E. *Global Studies: Europe.* Dubuque, IA: Dushkin/McGraw-Hill, 2003.

Goldman, Milton. *Revolution and Change in Central and Eastern Europe: Political, Economic, and Social Challenges.* Armonk, NY: M.E. Sharpe, 1997.

Gottman, Jean. *A Geography of Europe.* New York: Henry Holt, 1950.

Jordan-Bychkov, Terry, and Bella Bychkova-Jordan. *The European Culture Area.* New York: Rowman and Littlefield, 2001.

Masse, George L. *The Culture of Europe.* Boulder, CO: Westview Press, 1988.

McDonald, James R. *The European Scene: A Geographic Perspective.* Upper Saddle River, NJ: Prentice Hall, 1997.

Powell, John, ed. *Chronology of European History.* Pasadena, CA: Salem Press, 1997.

Schrier, Arnold et al. *Modern European Civilization.* Chicago: Scott, Foresman, 1963.

Unwin, Tim. *A European Geography.* Upper Saddle River, NJ: Prentice Hall, 1998.

Allport, Alan. *Austria*. Philadelphia: Chelsea House Publishers, 2002.

Allport, Alan. *England*. Philadelphia: Chelsea House Publishers, 2003.

Dendinger, Roger. *Scotland*. Philadelphia: Chelsea House Publishers, 2002.

Hogan Fouberg, Erin, and Edward P. Hogan. *Ireland*. Philadelphia: Chelsea House Publishers, 2003.

Hogan Fouberg, Erin, and Edward P. Hogan. *Norway*. Philadelphia: Chelsea House Publishers, 2004.

Horne, William R. *Germany*. Philadelphia: Chelsea House Publishers, 2003.

Jett, Stephen C. *France*. Philadelphia: Chelsea House Publishers, 2004.

Marran, James. *The Netherlands*. Philadelphia: Chelsea House Publishers, 2004.

Pavlović, Zoran. *Croatia*. Philadelphia: Chelsea House Publishers, 2002.

Pavlović, Zoran. *Italy*. Philadelphia: Chelsea House Publishers, 2003.

Pavlović, Zoran. *Turkey*. Philadelphia: Chelsea House Publishers, 2004.

Phillips, Douglas A. *Bosnia and Herzegovina*. Philadelphia: Chelsea House Publishers, 2004.

Sandness, Roger, and Charles F. Gritzner. *Iceland*. Philadelphia: Chelsea House Publishers, 2003.

117

ZORAN "ZOK" PAVLOVIĆ is a professional cultural geographer who works at Oklahoma State University. His previous contributions to Chelsea House series are *Republic of Georgia* (with Charles F. Gritzner), *Kazakhstan, Croatia, Italy,* and *Turkey*. When not conducting geographic research, Zok enjoys gourmet cooking, accompanied with a glass of good wine, and motorcycle travel. During his travels, he has visited numerous European countries. This book is a result of those travels.

CHARLES F. "FRITZ" GRITZNER is Distinguished Professor of Geography at South Dakota University in Brookings. He is now in his fifth decade of college teaching and research. During his career, he has taught more than 60 different courses, spanning the fields of physical, cultural, and regional geography. In addition to his teaching, he enjoys writing, working with teachers, and sharing his love for geography with students. As consulting editor for the MODERN WORLD NATIONS series, he has a wonderful opportunity to combine each of these "hobbies." Fritz has served as both President and Executive Director of the National Council for Geographic Education and has received the Council's highest honor, the George J. Miller Award for Distinguished Service. In March 2004, he won the Distinguished Teaching award from the Association of American Geographers at their annual meeting held in Philadelphia.